Men With Adult ADHD

How to Raise Emotionally Intelligent Men and Improve Relationships

Garth Zeus

© **Copyright 2023 - All rights reserved.**

The content contained within this book may not be reproduced, duplicated or transmitted without direct written permission from the author or the publisher.

Under no circumstances will any blame or legal responsibility be held against the publisher, or author, for any damages, reparation, or monetary loss due to the information contained within this book, either directly or indirectly.

Legal Notice:

This book is copyright protected. It is only for personal use. You cannot amend, distribute, sell, use, quote or paraphrase any part, or the content within this book, without the consent of the author or publisher.

Disclaimer Notice:

Please note the information contained within this document is for educational and entertainment purposes only. All effort has been executed to present accurate, up to date, reliable, complete information. No warranties of any kind are declared or implied. Readers acknowledge that the author is not engaged in the rendering of legal, financial, medical or professional advice. The content within this book has been derived from various sources. Please consult a licensed professional before attempting any techniques outlined in this book.

By reading this document, the reader agrees that under no circumstances is the author responsible for any losses, direct or indirect, that are incurred as a result of the use of the information contained within this document, including, but not limited to, errors, omissions, or inaccuracies.

Chapter 1:
An Introduction to ADHD

Dylan Rosen's story is not a happy one. He did well in elementary and middle school but found himself struggling when he reached high school. Dylan writes about how he drifted apart from his old friends and found it impossible to make new ones: "I viewed myself as a loner, a recluse. My confidence was slipping, and I had begun to experience the awful taste of depression" (Rosen & Pera, 2018).

Unfortunately, Dylan was not diagnosed with Attention Deficit/Hyperactivity Disorder (ADHD) in childhood. The condition was not well-known when he was a child, and his parents did not understand. He struggled with his report card and worried about how his parents would respond: "Cs were not good enough, even if I tried my best... My dad failed to see that I was trying... I felt shame and also felt like I was a disappointment" (Rosen & Pera, 2018).

Dylan's academic and home problems had a powerful effect on his self-esteem. He writes that "I felt worthless and alone at the age of 15. I would cry a lot because I was not good enough" (Rosen & Pera, 2018). His problems extended into community college, which he was unable to complete. By this point, he was severely depressed and anxious. Dylan couldn't hold down a job. He had married, but the marriage broke apart after three years.

Eventually, Dylan was diagnosed with ADHD by his therapist, who was treating him for his anxiety. The diagnosis came as a relief to Dylan, "like a traveling and parched nomad, finally finding a well in a barren desert" (Rosen & Pera, 2018). Since those years, his life has improved. He has gone back to college and gotten his degree. Yet the damage done by years of undiagnosed ADHD is still very painful: "I am an example of how doing your very best with what you have been given is still not good enough... I am constantly compensating for insecurities" (Rosen & Pera, 2018).

Not all ADHD stories are like this. This book aims to give practical advice and tips that might have helped Dylan with his struggles. The good news is that understanding ADHD is becoming increasingly common in our society. Though there remains some stigma and plenty of misperceptions, the old opines that ADHD "isn't real," or that medication should solve everything are becoming a thing of the ignorant past. Additionally, as ADHD becomes better known by the public, psychologists continue to learn more about the condition and how to manage its symptoms. Medication is just one half of the story: Research is constantly undertaken into other ways of managing ADHD symptoms, and how some people with ADHD can harness their neurodivergent brains in productive and positive ways.

Understanding the Nature of ADHD

But what is ADHD? If you've picked up this book, you probably have some preconceptions about it already. The stereotypical picture of an individual with ADHD is a ten-year-old boy fidgeting in class, unable to stop talking, and generally being disruptive. However, this does not reflect the broad class of people affected by ADHD. The American Psychiatric Association (n.d.) estimates that 8.4% of children and 2.5% of adults are affected by ADHD, whilst the National Institute of Mental Health (n.d.) notes that the condition is probably underdiagnosed, especially in girls and adults. As the stereotype for ADHD symptoms is disruptive behavior, it is less apparent in adults who are mature and have learned to curb disruptive behavior in the workplace and at home. Furthermore, many symptoms of ADHD overlap with the symptoms of other psychological disorders, further threatening to mask the condition and frustrate a diagnosis.

There are three types of ADHD: Predominantly inattentive type, predominantly hyperactive/impulsive type, and combined type. Combined type ADHD is the most common form of ADHD and includes symptoms of both predominantly inattentive type and predominantly hyperactive/impulsive type.

Meanwhile, predominantly inattentive type ADHD has symptoms related to—you guessed it—inattentiveness. This might present as difficulty remembering details about uninteresting subjects, excessive daydreaming, hyperfocus, and/or not looking at someone when they are talking to you. By comparison, predominantly hyperactive/impulsive type ADHD involves fidgeting, restlessness, excessive talking, interrupting, and risk-taking. The DSM-5 (2022), the modern diagnosis handbook used by psychologists today, provides more detail:

Symptoms of Inattentive Type	Symptoms of Hyperactive/ Impulsive Type
Often fails to pay close attention to details or makes careless mistakes at work or with other activities.	Often fidgets with hands or feet, or squirms when sitting.
Often has difficulty holding attention when performing tasks.	Often leaves their seat in situations where that is not expected.
Often doesn't seem to be listening when directly spoken to.	Often runs about where it is not appropriate to do so.
Often does not follow through on projects or instructions.	Often unable to participate in leisure activities quietly.
Often has difficulty organizing projects, tasks, and activities.	Is often driven as if "by a motor."
Often avoids or dislikes tasks that require sustained, mental effort.	Often talks excessively.
Often loses items that are necessary for certain tasks, like keys, eyeglasses, and so on.	Often blurts out an answer to a question before the question is completed.
Is often very distractible.	Often has difficulty waiting their turn.
Is often very forgetful in daily activities.	Often interrupts or intrudes on others who are busy with other activities.

The DSM-5 prescribes that a positive diagnosis of ADHD requires six symptoms from the table above when each symptom has been present for at least six months. If all the symptoms are symptoms of inattentive type, the diagnosis is inattentive type ADHD (the outdated term "ADD" referred to this type of ADHD). If all the symptoms are symptoms of hyperactivity/impulsive type, the diagnosis is hyperactive/impulsive type ADHD. If the symptoms are spread across the two columns, the diagnosis is combined type ADHD. Women with ADHD are more likely than men with ADHD to be diagnosed with inattentive type, whilst men with ADHD are more likely to be diagnosed with combined or hyperactive/impulsive type.

At present day, it is not possible to diagnose ADHD on the basis of a brain scan. Psychological clinicians will form a diagnosis by talking to you about your symptoms. They will assess whether your symptoms are persistent enough to meet the DSM-5 criteria and whether some symptoms were present in childhood as well.

ADHD is a behavioral condition, though this designator is becoming controversial. Some researchers now believe that it is a cognitive condition: More about how our brains are physically structured than our psychology. In Chapter 7, we will discuss this issue in more detail, but for now, it's worth knowing that ADHD is associated with lower levels of norepinephrine and dopamine. These are neurotransmitters, which means they are part of the process by which the brain sends signals to different parts of the brain and the body. This is a difference in brain chemistry. Additionally, there is good evidence to suggest differences in the ADHD brain when it comes to structure and function. Research finds that the amygdala and hippocampus–regions associated with emotional processing and impulsivity–are smaller in the brains of people with ADHD (Hoogman et al., 2017). Furthermore, there is evidence from modern imaging techniques that the ADHD brain has decreased brain activity in areas that control executive functions (Kim et al., 2010). The executive functions include planning, organizing, directing attention, memory, and emotional reactions. The ADHD brain is different, suggesting that the condition is cognitive rather than behavioral.

It can be tough living with a condition that affects your executive functions because it is harder to plan and organize your time. However, just because ADHD may be a cognitive rather than behavioral disorder, this doesn't mean that its symptoms cannot be managed with behavioral techniques. This book will outline strategies for boosting your executive functions, such as keeping a schedule, and little tips like where to put your keys and wallet. Especially in Chapter 6, we will see that impairment of executive functions can be managed and overcome.

What else is there to say about what ADHD is? Importantly, ADHD is considered a developmental disorder. This means that a positive diagnosis depends on at least some of your present symptoms also being presented in childhood. If you have ADHD, you may look back at your childhood and be able to recontextualize your behaviors as symptoms of ADHD. Did you struggle to pay attention in class? Were you talkative or restless? Were you always daydreaming? Many adults describe relief when they finally get their ADHD diagnosis in adulthood because it allows them to make sense of what's been happening to them their entire life.

Comparing Children With ADHD to Adults With ADHD

As noted, when most people think of ADHD, they tend to think about overt, hyperactive symptoms. A young boy in class may fidget or blurt out what they are thinking. However, this does not reflect how adults (or young girls) will typically present symptoms of ADHD. Adult men with ADHD are less likely to start running about a room because we have learned and internalized that this is disruptive behavior in most settings. If you have not been diagnosed as a child, an adult with ADHD may have instinctively put in place methods of managing their symptoms that further mask a diagnosis.

For example, a common sign of ADHD in adult men is visiting the bathroom at work more often than most. Men with ADHD don't do this because their condition causes them to need the toilet more: Instead, they do it so they can stretch their legs and alleviate some of their restlessness. This is a symptom of hyperactiveness, but it is less obvious than a young boy running around a classroom or climbing up onto his desk. These men have learned to deal with their hyperactiveness in a way that causes minimal disruption to anyone else.

Here's another example of a hyperactive/impulsive symptom: Difficulty waiting your turn. This symptom gets to the feeling of impatience, which can be a core component of ADHD. However, adults know that it is antisocial and disruptive to cut in line or to take your turn in a board game out of order. As such, many adults with ADHD repress this behavior. But impatience comes out in different ways. Men with ADHD often demonstrate irritability and mood swings and might have a quick temper. They are less able to deal with stress and frustration because they are less patient as a result of their ADHD (Adamis et al., 2022). Furthermore, because male aggression is sometimes tolerated in society–seen as a fundamental facet of *maleness*–men can exhibit these symptoms and not realize that they are symptoms of ADHD. Orlov (2022) notes that "fewer men [than women] with ADHD see their anger and rage as a problem."

Adult men with ADHD have been living with the condition their entire life. This means that—even if they don't realize they have ADHD–men have put in place coping methods and strategies for managing their symptoms. This can result in behaviors that further mask ADHD symptoms, exacerbated by gender differences (whether these differences are the result of biological sex or societal gender norms). Orlov (2022) notes that research "suggests that men have greater difficulty recovering from conflict than women do." After a conflict, a man's blood pressure remains elevated for longer. Why is this relevant to ADHD? Because ADHD can often cause conflict, and elevated blood pressure is physically uncomfortable. Men with ADHD have gone through their lives getting into misunderstandings and conflicts because of the symptoms of their ADHD, and they have learned that this makes them feel physically uncomfortable. In response, many men with ADHD use avoidance behavior to avoid conflict, such as trying to lie their way out of trouble or being emotionally distant in a relationship. This can badly affect relationships, and also mask symptoms of ADHD: By being emotionally distant, we hide our frustrations and impatience from others. In Chapter 5, we will think more about the pressures that ADHD can put on your relationships and social interactions and look at some strategies for meeting these difficulties directly.

Looking After Yourself

In Chapter 3, we will talk more about symptoms of ADHD in adults, and how to recognize the condition in yourself and others. For now, it is important to recognize that ADHD is a multifaceted condition that does not correspond to many people's preconceptions. Though this book will touch on how ADHD is typically experienced by a wide range of people, it focuses on the experience of adult men. We will consider strategies for identifying bad habits—such as avoidance behaviors we have just discussed—that you may have instinctively put in place to deal with undiagnosed ADHD. These bad habits are perfectly understandable and demonstrate self-awareness and self-reliance. Unfortunately, though, they are not always healthy and productive. In addition to tackling these bad habits, we'll also consider handy tips and strategies for managing symptoms of ADHD: Such as methods to organize your space, deal with clutter, and manage your time effectively.

We will also discuss some of the dangers associated with ADHD, especially for adult men. Some of these are direct dangers related to symptoms of ADHD. For example, though impulsivity can sometimes be a positive and life-affirming instinct, sometimes it can get you into trouble or lead you into danger. The website NeuroHealth (n.d.) notes that a common sign of ADHD in adults is speeding, which of course brings physical danger to yourself and others. However, other risks associated with ADHD are comorbidities. A comorbid condition of ADHD is a condition that you are more likely to have if you have ADHD. Unfortunately, a host of psychological disorders are comorbid with ADHD, the most common being bipolar disorder, cyclothymia (mild mood swings relating to energy level), depression, anxiety, and self-harm. In Chapter 4, we will discuss this topic in more detail, and discuss how some conditions might actually be *caused* by ADHD. For example, many men base their self-worth on their job performance, whether rightly or wrongly. Given that the symptoms of ADHD can result in problems at work, it follows that ADHD can create situations that negatively affect your self-esteem. This can lead to depression. Tragically, research in Sweden has found that people with

ADHD are ten times as likely to commit suicide as individuals who do not have ADHD (0.2%, against 0.02%) (Phillips, 2018).

However, you should not be fearful. By picking up this book, you have already shown a willingness to tackle your or a loved one's ADHD head-on. By managing your symptoms, you can directly improve your life and live productively and happily. In Chapter 4, we will even discuss how ADHD, when properly managed, can be your personal superpower. If you can learn to harness your hyperfocus and hyperactiveness into productive ends, you will find yourself capable of feats of productivity that will amaze others. Moreover, by embracing intrusive thoughts in the right contexts, you can make the most of your innate creativity and unique problem-solving skills.

Furthermore, you needn't feel alone. In Chapter 2, we'll discuss in more detail what it feels like to have ADHD and share stories of people who live with the condition. ADHD is increasingly common due to improved diagnostic tools. We live in a neurodiverse world. Though ADHD comes with disadvantages, those symptoms can be managed, and we should not discount the advantages as well. The sheer variety of the abilities of our species is something to be celebrated: As long as we can organize ourselves as a society by our strengths and passions, we can do amazing things. People with ADHD have impressive skills to offer the workplace and the world, and that shouldn't be overlooked.

It's also worth stating, right from the offset, that ADHD is not related in any way to intelligence. That means that having ADHD does not mean you are dumb, nor does it mean you are smart. There are people with ADHD who are geniuses, and there are people with ADHD who are very much not! If you have ADHD, your condition does not define you. It may be a part of who you are (and I hope you can learn to accept or even celebrate that), but it is not the *entirety* of who you are.

You may have come to this book after being diagnosed in adulthood. That's more than okay. James Bloodworth, a journalist, and writer in the United Kingdom was also diagnosed in adulthood. If you're like him, you may look back on your childhood and see all the familiar signs of ADHD. James notes that he always had trouble concentrating in school: "This led to frustration and mounting disciplinary issues as the years went by" (Bloodworth, 2021). Even though James found school difficult, his problems worsened when he left the helpful relative structure of the high school environment. He struggled to hold down a job.

Eventually, after a series of struggles, James returned to his passion for writing and politics. He returned to college, and then to university. He achieved what he humbly refers to as a "modicum" (Bloodworth, 2021) of success. James didn't yet realize he had ADHD, even though his productivity felt erratic: "I could produce good work when I was able to summon the power to sit down at my computer and write, yet my ability to do so was sporadic and unpredictable" (Bloodworth, 2021). In a word, he was able to *function*, which probably masked his underlying ADHD for so long. But there were issues. James found himself missing deadlines seemingly at random, after sleeping for less than eight hours the night before or eating poorly. When he came across the symptoms of ADHD on the internet, he realized that he recognized the symptoms in himself.

Though James's doctor was less than helpful, James was able to see an online ADHD assessment and secure his diagnosis. Now that he is diagnosed, he is able to treat his condition both with medication and management strategies. James describes it as amazing (Bloodworth, 2021):

> Work is much easier and I'm more productive than at any time in my entire life. Many of the coping strategies I once used to deal with my ADHD–such as binge eating and excessive social media use–have melted away since I started taking medication. Moreover, for the first time in my life, I feel I can sit and relax without the need for constant stimulation (para. 12).

You may recognize yourself in James's story. Alternatively–or additionally–you may see yourself in Dylan's. Either way, you are welcome here. ADHD is a lifetime condition, but it is very treatable. And I don't just mean that it is treatable with medication. I recognize that medication for ADHD can often come with unpleasant side effects, such as trouble sleeping, loss of appetite, headaches, and stomachaches. Others report that the medication can make them feel less like themselves. Phillips (2018) puts it starkly, reflecting on his experiences with ADHD medication as a student: "You can either get better grades easier and lose part of yourself, or you can be who you are be crucified for it in the grade book." If you are struggling with your medication, this book aims to offer alternative ways to manage your symptoms and live a happier life. Of course, that is not to say that you should stop taking your medication if it is working for you. The strategies and tips in this book are effective supplements to stimulant and non-stimulant medication.

Ultimately, just as ADHD itself is broad, people with ADHD know that medication is not the whole picture for everyone. Medication can be enormously effective, but it is unlikely to deal with all your symptoms. For example, Kendra, interviewed by Thriving With ADHD (n.d.), notes that medication has been "life-changing" when it comes to giving her focus, but has done nothing for her memory. Different people with ADHD are going to have different experiences, and that's okay. This book aims to give helpful advice to everyone, whether it is supplementing stimulant drugs or not. Simple advice like maintaining a nutritious diet, or practicing good sleep hygiene, can be a huge part of managing your ADHD as an adult man.

This relates to an important general point: We are not all the same. Though hyperactive/impulsive type ADHD is more common in men than inattentive type ADHD, this does not mean that there are no men struggling with inattention. Many conditions are comorbid with ADHD, but that doesn't mean that you're going to suffer from depression if you have ADHD. Embrace your uniqueness, and feel free to pick and choose from the strategies and tips that will help *you*.

Relatedly, ADHD can affect different parts of your life, and, for some people, certain areas of life are affected more than others. ADHD symptoms can affect a relationship because inattentiveness can be confused with not caring, and an inability to follow through and complete tasks can be frustrating for your partner. It can also affect your work, because you may find yourself distracted from your work, or unable to plan out and finish a project. This book will offer advice for all areas of life. The truth is

You may be wondering how ADHD can affect some parts of your life and not others. The truth is that ADHD probably does affect every part of your life, but some of your instinctive coping strategies have been more successful than others. For example, a lot of the pressure ADHD may put on your work life can be alleviated by finding the right career. People with ADHD are disproportionately represented among entrepreneurs because we naturally gravitate to jobs that are flexible enough to accommodate dramatic shifts in productivity. Being your own boss can avoid many of the common work issues other people with ADHD face. Similarly, if you have a particularly patient and organized partner, you may find that your relationship is less affected by your ADHD symptoms. In particular, people with ADHD tend to struggle with day-to-day chores. This difficulty might not be relevant to your life, however, if you are married to a homemaker. Over the course of this book, you may realize that you have made choices and decisions that help manage your ADHD symptoms without meaning to. This is to be celebrated: Instinctively, you have known what lifestyle works for you, and you have worked towards it. That isn't to say, however, that this book can't still offer some useful tips for rounding off the edges.

With that in mind, we should get started. It's time to learn more about the experience of having ADHD, and how your symptoms can be managed and even harnessed for positive effects

.

Chapter 2:
The Exploding ADHD Mind

Ren, aged 38, first learned more about ADHD when his best friend's son was diagnosed with the condition. As he learned more about the condition, he began to see similarities between the symptoms described and his own life: "I began to suspect my own struggle to thrive may have been due to a deeper cause. That maybe I wasn't just lazy, crazy, and stupid" (Thriving With ADHD, n.d.).

Like many people with undiagnosed ADHD, Ren had struggled at school. His grades didn't reflect what he knew his capabilities to be, and he struggled with focus and inattentiveness in boring classes. These difficulties followed him into adult life, where "full-time jobs always felt suffocating which led to depression" (Thriving With ADHD, n.d.). Ren also had difficulties in his relationships and personal life. He describes how he found it difficult to regulate his emotions, and how the smallest upset could provoke a spiral of explosive anger and self-hate.

Ren was diagnosed with ADHD in adulthood. Since being diagnosed, he has enrolled in an education program equivalent to completing 12th grade in high school and has then gone on to graduate with a Bachelor of Environmental Science. Ren credits some of this to his ADHD medication but notes that the medication "hasn't cured my condition. At night when my medication wears off, all my symptoms reappear" (Thriving With ADHD, n.d.). He still has to manage his symptoms and deal with the struggle of ADHD, but the diagnosis has been fundamental to his self-perception: "What my diagnosis has changed for me is my self-worth and self-esteem which has led to a mentally healthier, more stable and equally able life" (Thriving With ADHD, n.d.).

Difficulty with regulating emotions is especially common in adult men with ADHD. However, many men don't realize that their patterns of behavior are symptomatic of an underlying condition. Michael, aged 33, thought of himself as a normal, functioning person for much of his life. He acknowledged that he was prone to excessive talking or losing focus, but he could hold down a job and his life was largely in order. However, as the difficulties of undiagnosed ADHD piled up, things started to become more chaotic. Michael found that he was having trouble getting to sleep. His vision was starting to blur when he tried to concentrate. He began to have difficulties maintaining relationships, and his short-term memory started to let him down. Tellingly, he also became more emotional, unable to stop small frustrations from exploding into sudden anger.

These symptoms led Michael to seek help from his doctors, who soon diagnosed him with ADHD. Since then, Michael has found himself better able to manage his symptoms with medication. His journey with diagnosed ADHD has just begun, but already "it's been a bit of a roller coaster ride getting used to [...] not living with the brain fog and accepting I require medication to think more clearly" (Thriving With ADHD, n.d.).

Causes of ADHD

As ADHD becomes a better-known condition in wider society, diagnoses are increasing rapidly. As schools get better at recognizing ADHD symptoms in their pupils, adults are learning about the condition when their children are diagnosed. And, because ADHD has a genetic factor, it is no surprise that parents of children with ADHD are now discovering that they might have ADHD as well. But what causes ADHD?

As we discussed in the last chapter, it is controversial whether ADHD is a behavioral or a cognitive condition. New research increasingly demonstrates that the ADHD brain is different structurally, functionally, and chemically. The NHS (2021) adds that there is likely to be a genetic component to ADHD, such that you are more likely to be diagnosed with ADHD if someone else in your family has been diagnosed with the condition. Nonetheless, the causes of ADHD are not fully understood. The NHS (2021) notes that some statistical correlations suggest some factors in the cause of ADHD: For example, ADHD is more commonly diagnosed in people who were born prematurely, were born with low birth weight, or had mothers who smoked or abused drugs during their pregnancy.

Importantly, though, there is no established link between parenting styles and a later diagnosis of ADHD. You do not have ADHD because you were given too much freedom as a child, or because you weren't properly disciplined. These stigmas that are sometimes associated with ADHD are simply not based in fact.

Looking Back

If you are an adult with undiagnosed ADHD, you may have found coping mechanisms and ways to function over the years. This can frustrate a diagnosis of ADHD. This is what happened to Zoe Rose, who was diagnosed with ADHD at 38. Like Michael, Zoe considered herself to be functioning well. Nogrady (2022) writes that "she was an adult woman with a great job, a stable marriage, and was successfully parenting a child. She didn't feel at all like the stereotype of the 10-year-old boy who can't sit still in class." However, Zoe didn't realize that she had structured her life in a way that implicitly helped to manage her symptoms of ADHD. She was married to a partner who was willing and capable to take care of mundane, day-to-day tasks around the household, while she focused on her career. In other words, her partner was completing the tasks that someone with ADHD would find particularly challenging.

Zoe was diagnosed with ADHD after her partner fell ill. Because her partner couldn't undertake the mundane, day-to-day tasks anymore, Zoe had to fill in and found it extremely difficult to do so. Suddenly, the life Zoe had implicitly structured to help manage her symptoms of ADHD was gone, and Zoe found herself struggling. Though a diagnosis of ADHD didn't magically fix Zoe's symptoms, it did give much-needed context to her struggles, helping Zoe understand herself and her life.

You may recognize yourself in some of these stories. You may look back at your childhood and realize that you were struggling with the symptoms of ADHD all throughout school. Alternatively, you might look back on your life and suddenly recognize all the subtle steps you took to manage your symptoms without realizing it. For example, maybe you found yourself gravitating to a fast-paced, high-intensity job that has helped you maintain focus and attention throughout your career. The website adda (n.d.) notes that jobs in the emergency services, like doctors, police officers, and firefighters, are disproportionately represented by people with ADHD. Maybe you've become your own boss, so you can work to your own schedule of sudden bursts and lulls of productivity. Outside of your work life, you might have put in place strategies for managing your time and organizing your life. For example, you might swear by your day planner, or have married someone who implicitly helps you structure out your day.

In Chapter 3, we will consider useful habits that can help you manage your symptoms of ADHD. Additionally, in Chapter 5, we'll consider strategies for maintaining relationships with ADHD, and, in Chapter 6, we will look at specific techniques for managing your space. In the meantime, it's worth taking this time to reflect and identify habits you have already put in place as an adult man with ADHD. It's okay if you can't recognize any habits: After all, this book is here to provide useful tips and strategies that will help you manage your symptoms. However, if you do recognize some implicit strategies that you already have in place, it's worth reflecting on them and objectively evaluating them. Maybe it's worth expanding some helpful strategies. For example, you might maintain a very structured schedule at work to help you manage projects and complete tasks. If you're finding this successful, but you're struggling to complete household tasks, you might consider expanding your work schedule to incorporate your entire day.

On the other hand, when reflecting on the implicit strategies you've put in place to manage your ADHD symptoms, you might realize that some strategies are counterproductive. For example, in the last chapter, we discussed how some men with ADHD become emotionally distant as a means of managing their feelings of frustration and emotional dysregulation. This is a perfectly understandable response to the unpleasantness of frustration and conflict, and you shouldn't beat yourself up if you have resorted to avoidance behaviors. After all, being emotionally distant probably *has* helped you avoid some conflicts. However, being emotionally distant is not the best way to deal with emotional dysregulation. Though it may avoid an argument in the short term, your partner may misunderstand your behaviors as uncaring or cruel.

By reflecting on some implicit strategies and honestly appraising them, you can wean yourself off some of the less healthy strategies you have put in place. For example, if you do find yourself lying or being emotionally distant as a way to avoid conflict, it's important to come to grips with that and consider other ways of managing your frustration. Sometimes, it can be a very important step to simply tell your partner about how you're feeling. If you let your partner understand your patterns of behavior, you can avoid them thinking that you are uninterested or uncaring about them. That's an excellent first step to improving your relationship.

Consider Phillip, a married man with two children. Before his ADHD diagnosis, his marriage was under a lot of pressure. He would forget to turn up to important family events, like his son's sports day. He would forget birthdays and anniversaries and leave household projects half-completed. Meanwhile, his wife was struggling and becoming frustrated: "His wife complained that with him, she had three kids to look after, not two. He knew he would often forget to do his share of the household chores and didn't pull his weight at home" (Adult ADHD Clinic, n.d.). Additionally, when Philip tried to discuss his perspective, he would struggle to express himself and drift off on conversational tangents.

Philip's symptoms of ADHD caused tension in his marriage. To help manage this stress, Philip "was constantly staying up late at night playing online games, as he felt it was the only way he could relax" (Adult ADHD Clinic, n.d.). Implicitly, Philip had put in place a strategy for managing his symptoms. Unfortunately, this strategy was not particularly healthy. Because he was staying up late at night, he was tired the next day, no doubt exacerbating his distractibility and lack of focus. It also added further stress on his marriage, because his wife saw him playing games and concluded that he was choosing to avoid his responsibilities. Ultimately, he had put in place a coping strategy that was doing more harm than good.

Fortunately, Philip's story has a happy ending. He was diagnosed with ADHD and was able to receive treatment that has avoided "a few near misses" (Adult ADHD Clinic, n.d.) in his marriage. The diagnosis has provided huge relief, and he has been able to reflect on his patterns of behavior to identify what is helpful and what is unhealthy.

Have you experienced something similar? Maybe you find yourself disappearing into your own hobbies as a way of avoiding conflict in your relationships. If you do so, consider whether this coping strategy is effective or counterproductive. Of course, there's nothing wrong with having interests and passions. An outlet can be immensely helpful, both in managing your stress and maintaining healthy relationships. On the other hand, if it has started to become an avoidance tactic, your pattern of behavior may be doing more harm than good.

The Power of Self-Awareness

Everyone—whether they present symptoms of ADHD or not—can benefit from observing their own patterns of behavior. By recognizing triggers and patterns that are less healthy, we can all take sensible steps to improve our lives. Of course, however, it is particularly important if you have been diagnosed with ADHD, because there is more of a necessity to put strategies in place to manage your symptoms. Think of it this way: When forming a strategy for anything in life, it's important to be as informed as possible to make sure that strategy is a success. A strategy for a project that overlooks obvious complications and potential flaws is not a particularly good strategy. The same applies to strategies for managing your symptoms of ADHD. The only difference is that it's *your* behavioral patterns and triggers that you need to be informed about.

You may find that a little self-reflection can be incredibly empowering. Understanding your own triggers and patterns of behavior can be a little bit like a superpower: Allowing you to control and harness your psychology for a happier, more productive life. If you have ADHD, you can also look at your patterns of behavior to gain a better understanding of your condition.

In the last chapter, we noted that there are broadly three types of ADHD: Predominantly inattentive type, predominantly hyperactive/impulsive type, and combined type. When reflecting on your own patterns of behavior, you may be able to recognize the exact variant of your condition. For example, when you procrastinate—and we all do it—what form does your procrastination take? It may be that you excessively daydream or get distracted by tangential subjects that swallow up your time and attention. If so, you are exhibiting more of the symptoms of predominantly inattentive type. This is important because your type of ADHD informs what strategies are likely to be helpful. For example, if you're struggling to keep your focus on a big project, you can use the Pomodoro Technique. The Pomodoro Technique asks you to commit to focusing on your project for twenty-five minutes, and then to break for five minutes. This is one "cycle." After the 5-minute break, you then commit to another cycle. After four cycles, you then take a longer, 15 or 30-minute break. The Pomodoro Technique is effective because it only commits you to

25 minutes of focus at a time. Use of a timer (a simple Google of "Pomodoro Technique timer" will find plenty of websites to help you) can help you cut through distractions, interrupting a procrastinating daydream or tangential rabbit hole.

By contrast, let's consider another way that you might procrastinate. Maybe you visit the bathroom, even though you don't need the toilet. You might find yourself excessively fidgeting or tapping your foot against the floor. Alternatively, you may find that you procrastinate by starting a conversation with your work neighbor, enthusiastically chatting away while your project gathers dust. If this describes your own patterns of behavior, you are exhibiting symptoms of hyperactivity/impulsive type ADHD. Again, this can inform your strategies a little better. Think about when you are at your most productive or when you are most likely to procrastinate. You might find that you are more productive after lunch–especially if you are a little more active at lunch. If you can incorporate physical exercise (even if it's just a brisk walk) into your routine, you might find yourself less likely to procrastinate. Furthermore, the Pomodoro Technique can also be used with hyperactivity or impulsiveness in mind. In the five-minute breaks, you may find it effective to get up from your chair and stretch your legs or use a fidget spinner to keep your hands busy. You might try to limit visits to the water cooler for those five-minute windows, to avoid interrupting your focused time.

Most people with ADHD, of course, present symptoms of combined type. This means that you will have symptoms both of inattentive type and hyperactive/impulsive type. However, this doesn't mean that you can't tailor strategies to your specific symptoms. For example, you may have combined type ADHD but not demonstrate any fidgeting or restlessness. Remember that being diagnosed with combined type ADHD doesn't mean that you have *all* the symptoms of inattentive type, and *all* the symptoms of hyperactive/impulsive type: You will have a scattering of symptoms from one type, and a scattering of symptoms from another. If you don't tend to feel restless or fidget, your strategies for managing your productivity should focus less on physical activity.

Though it is important to understand your particular type of ADHD when thinking about yourself and potential strategies for managing your symptoms, it's okay to think at the level of symptoms alone. If you're distracted at work and express this by being a bit of a chatterbox, you might find it tremendously helpful to talk to your employer about finding a quieter place to do your work: Perhaps a quiet room, or even just a corner seat in the office. If your main problem is distractibility, then it may be helpful to see if it's possible to program your phone so that all calls go directly to voicemail. You can schedule a time to go through your messages later in the day. Ultimately, by understanding yourself, you can tailor strategies to maximally help you.

Self-understanding can also bring with it psychological relief. Many people who were diagnosed with ADHD later in their lives describe the profound relief of their diagnosis. Clinton, aged 37, was diagnosed with ADHD at the age of 24. For him, "it was like the missing piece of a jigsaw fell into place. Everything made sense" (Thriving With ADHD, n.d.). Similarly, Jo, aged 35, was diagnosed at the age of 28: "With my diagnosis came an enormous sense of relief. I'd struggled my whole life with things no one else seemed to struggle with. I'd been labeled as lazy and had started to believe it myself" (Thriving With ADHD, n.d.).

There is a reason that "what x are you?" quizzes on Buzzfeed are so popular. As human beings, we take pleasure and relief from categorizing and understanding our own nature. All of us are interested in our own patterns of behavior. With that in mind, really take the time to think about your own behavioral patterns. This is your excuse to indulge: Not only is self-reflection fulfilling in itself, but you will be able to use your insights to manage the symptoms of your ADHD and live a happier, more fulfilling life.

To help you monitor your patterns of behavior and keep track of your triggers, you may find it enormously helpful to journal. There are many ways to journal, from pen and paper to apps designed to illuminate your psychological behaviors. Finch (2017) recommends the Grid Diary app. Grid Diary presents each day in a grid, with each box presenting a different prompt to answer: Examples include asking about your general mood or to describe the weather. You can customize these prompts to whatever you'd like and break down your day into different aspects that can really help expose your triggers for certain behaviors. Over time, you may realize that patterns emerge. For example, consider customizing one of the prompts to ask you about your sleep patterns. Over a few months, you may find that there is a powerful link between how well you slept to how distractible you feel the next day. It can be very helpful to have this record in black and white, so you can identify patterns and learn facets of yourself that would otherwise be obscured by the mess of daily life.

Self-reflection and journaling can also be a great way of charting your attention levels over a day. Dan Martell is a tech entrepreneur, investor, and speaker with ADHD (and also a millionaire). He considers energy management to be a key part of his management of ADHD symptoms. By reflecting on his patterns of behavior, Dan has found that he does his best work in the morning: His energy levels are high, he can focus better, and is more productive. Having learned this about himself, Dan has decided to schedule all of his meetings in the afternoon, so that his morning time can be dedicated to tasks that require close focus and attention (Martell, 2018).

Of course, Dan Martell has the advantage of being his own boss. He can choose when to schedule his meetings. However, even if you're not so lucky, you can exhibit some control over your schedule. Most of us have multiple tasks that we need to do in a given day and some discretion over how they are ordered. With that in mind, think about your energy patterns and how best to structure your time. For example, maybe you always come back particularly focused after lunch: Perhaps you exhibit symptoms of hyperactive/impulsive type ADHD, and having a little walk outside does wonders for your attention levels. You may find it helpful to schedule complex, detail-oriented tasks for the early afternoon because that's when you'll have maximal focus. Alternatively, like Dan, you might find yourself maximally productive in the morning: If that's the case, schedule tasks that need your close attention for the first thing in the workday, and schedule less detail-oriented tasks for the afternoon. Of course, these insights don't need to be relegated to your work life alone. If, upon self-reflection, you realize you're a bit of a night owl, why not get your paperwork done on Sunday evening and leave Sunday morning for rest and relaxation?

Being aware of your own patterns of behavior is especially useful if you're taking medication for ADHD, because you may find that when you take medication is very important to the management of your symptoms. Do you remember Ren from before? He detailed how his medication can wear off at night, leading to a reemergence of his symptoms. By being aware of this, Ren can plan accordingly and put helpful strategies into place to manage his condition. Furthermore, understanding how your medication is affecting you is very important when it comes to discussing your medication with your doctor. It can help you identify with your doctor whether your medication is working for you, or whether the dosage needs to be amended.

Relief and Regret

Once you've been diagnosed with ADHD and begun to reflect on your own patterns of behavior, you can recontextualize events in your life and start to understand yourself a little better. As noted, this can often bring with it an enormous sense of relief. However, if you're like many other people with ADHD, you might have experienced that relief fading, to be replaced with feelings of sadness or grief. Though Jo felt relief after her diagnosis of ADHD, she began to think about what could have been if she had been diagnosed sooner: "I ... felt sad that I hadn't been diagnosed earlier, as maybe my life wouldn't have been so hard. Maybe I'd have achieved more?"

These feelings of regret are very common in people who have been diagnosed with ADHD later in life. If you are experiencing this feeling, you are not alone. Feelings of grief for what could have been are very natural, and shouldn't be ignored or bottled up. It's always helpful to be honest with yourself about how you're feeling and to open up to others if you can.

Kelvin Blunt was diagnosed with ADHD at age 49 and notes that "it was by happenstance that I learned of my ADHD" (Blunt, 2022). Kelvin had been visiting a therapist but, when the Covid-19 pandemic hit, found that he couldn't get through to his regular therapist on the phone. This led to him speaking to a new therapist that suddenly wanted to focus on some of Kelvin's specific symptoms: In particular, how Kelvin often experienced restlessness. Kelvin writes that "with each question, I fought a floodgate of tears. I answered as if I was meeting myself for the first time" (Blunt, 2022).

Kelvin was diagnosed with ADHD, and, like many people diagnosed with ADHD in adulthood, felt the relief of finally understanding what was happening to him in his life. He felt grateful. However, he "experienced intense grief in the couple of months after my diagnosis ... a treasure trove of what-ifs, discoveries, and regrets flooded my mind" (Blunt, 2022). He realized that his deceased mother had suffered from ADHD. He was able to understand why he had struggled throughout his life, but this "brought more anguish than closure" (Blunt, 2022). After all, had Kelvin been diagnosed sooner, perhaps many aspects of his life would have been different. Maybe he would have struggled less or found more success. These feelings are natural. However, as Kelvin himself writes, "I knew it best not to get stuck in a rabbit hole of regret" (Blunt, 2022). It was important for him to discuss these feelings and work through them with his therapist. If you have been diagnosed with ADHD later in life and are experiencing grief or regret, it may also be worth talking to a therapist about how you're feeling. Just remember—to belabor the point—that these feelings are natural and normal.

ADHD is a lifetime condition, but the symptoms of the condition are manageable. This book will provide many strategies that can supplement your medication and help you to live your best life with ADHD. However, ultimately, it is *you* that will truly make the difference. To choose the best strategies and determine the right dosage of medication, there is no substitute for self-reflection and self-knowledge. So, take the time today: Now, even. Think about your patterns of behavior, whether they are positive or harmful, occasional or sustained. Use journaling or bespoke apps to aid you in finding your triggers and use that knowledge to help you in your ADHD journey. Though it can be painful, and even scary, you will thank yourself in the long run.

Chapter 3:
Managing Your Symptoms

Rick Green is a comedy writer, actor, and director. Like many people diagnosed with ADHD in adulthood, he first learned about the condition when his son was diagnosed with the condition. Bailey (2022) tells his story: "When the doctor ticked off the symptoms, [Rick] was surprised and confused. 'I thought everyone is like this,' he said, assuming the rest of the world struggled with lateness, forgetfulness, difficulty following through, and paying attention."

When Rick was diagnosed with ADHD, he was aged 47. When he looked back at his life, suddenly a lot of his struggles made sense: "One day a light bulb went on: 'No wonder I was able to write thousands of short skits but could never finish a single screenplay.' Later, came 'Wow, medication really helps!' Which quickly turned to 'Damn, if I'd only known sooner, I could have written movies!'" (Bailey, 2022).

Unfortunately, Rick's "family dismissed his diagnosis" (Bailey, 2022). But Rick wasn't to be put off, and with behavioral techniques and medication, started to manage his symptoms. Finding success with his treatment, he started making videos to explain what ADHD is: "While his videos started from a place of anger, he now makes them from the perspective of love" (Bailey, 2022).

Rick's story encapsulates many of the difficulties and feelings that come with a diagnosis of ADHD in adulthood. He experienced the relief of the diagnosis, the recontextualization and understanding of his own life, as well as the grief and regret that comes from not having been diagnosed earlier. Additionally, Rick's story includes him running into the stigma of ADHD and being confronted with those misperceptions that others often make when you tell them about your diagnosis.

Misconceptions About ADHD

The stigma of ADHD, and the misperceptions that follow, are happily becoming less common as society learns more about the condition. However, there are still people who scoff at the very existence of ADHD as a mental disorder. For every person who offers empathy and understanding, there will be another person who just thinks the ten-year-old boy with ADHD is badly behaved, or that the adult man who never finishes a project is lazy. These misconceptions are often hurtful, especially if it comes from someone you love. However, if you can, it can be empowering to show them the empathy that they have denied you. To some extent, we can understand where the misconceptions arise. Many of the symptoms of ADHD are frustrating to the people in our lives, regardless of their source. It can be difficult to live with someone with ADHD because it *is* annoying that we don't finish a household chore or need constant help with time management.

However, just because we can empathize with our loved ones, this doesn't mean that their misconceptions are correct. Ultimately, ADHD is a neurological disorder. Your ADHD does not make you lazy, uncaring, or stupid, and it can be very painful to have to explain that to someone who you would otherwise expect to support and love you. Your empathy doesn't commit you to putting yourself down. We can understand that they are frustrated and try to communicate and explain the reality of ADHD, but sometimes, tragically, the people in our lives just don't want to listen.

Of course, the stigma of ADHD isn't relegated to our friends and family. As ADHD becomes better known as a condition, the myth of its nonexistence has been replaced with the myth of its overdiagnosis. Children and teenagers experimenting with their self-identity talk about undiagnosed conditions on social media apps like TikTok, eliciting eye rolls from skeptical types in the media. It is a common refrain that doctors are too quick to diagnose mental disorders and too quick to prescribe medication. Even if you have some sympathy for the idea that medications are too quickly prescribed, this does not mean that your own ADHD is wrongly diagnosed, or that your medication isn't an absolute lifesaver. Unfortunately, people with ADHD quickly have to develop a thick skin.

The good news is that, on the whole, things are improving. The idea that ADHD is overdiagnosed is less harmful than the idea that ADHD is a made-up condition. As a society, we seem to be going in the right direction. Moreover, regardless of ignorance and prejudice, the reality of our conditions is supported by the medical profession and the law. Noor (n.d.) notes that ADHD "is covered under both the Rehabilitation Act of 1973, section 504, and the Americans with Disabilities Act (ADA). This means that an employer cannot discriminate against someone with ADHD and must provide reasonable accommodations in the workplace." Even if your boss is ignorant, they have legal obligations if your ADHD has a significant impact on your ability to do your job.

In the meantime, it is important not to internalize the stigma and the misconceptions. What I said above bears repeating: Your ADHD does not mean that you are lazy, uncaring, or stupid. Many people with ADHD are trying a lot harder than others. Though it can be hard, and it can be hurtful, try not to take ignorant statements to heart, and try to explain your perspective to others who don't understand, especially friends and family. If you can do this calmly and with empathy, it is ultimately their shortcoming if they choose not to listen.

Adult Symptoms of ADHD

Throughout this book, we have noted that the overt symptoms of a typical ten-year-old boy with ADHD do not necessarily mirror how ADHD presents in adult men. This variance can produce further misconceptions and can also make it difficult to recognize symptoms in yourself or others. Ho & Kittleson (2022) describe nine "hidden" signs of ADHD that are common in adults with inattentive type ADHD:

1. You often make careless mistakes or lack attention to detail. Though this may seem more overt, the crucial thing is that this symptom may be disguised by your preferences. Many adults with undiagnosed ADHD will avoid detail-oriented tasks, instead choosing to focus on the "big picture." If this describes you, it's worth reflecting on why you avoid detail-oriented tasks. If it's because you find them particularly difficult, this could be a sign of adult ADHD.

2. You have difficulty sustaining your attention. Because adults have the ability to organize their lives around topics that interest them, this symptom can sometimes be hidden. If you have the power to avoid tasks and topics that don't interest you, you may not realize that you have severe difficulty sustaining your attention when it comes to boring activities.

3. You don't seem to listen when you're spoken to directly. Have you ever realized that someone was talking to you at the end of their sentence, and asked them to repeat themselves? It is not uncommon for people with ADHD to be informally diagnosed as having hearing difficulties by their friends and family. If you don't think your hearing is impaired, but you always need your partner to repeat themselves, this may be a hidden sign of ADHD.

4. You have difficulty following through on tasks or instructions. Again, this can be less obvious in adults because adults have more control over their activities. A child is assigned projects by their teachers or by their parents, but an adult (outside of their work) can abandon a household project with relatively less accountability. If you are constantly

abandoning DIY projects, or always starting something new, this may be something to think about.

5. You have poor organizational skills. If you live alone, this may be a tricky symptom to spot, because the only person being affected is yourself. Furthermore, it's all too easy to confuse severe difficulties between being organized and being generally scatterbrained. If your poor organizational skills are negatively affecting your work and relationships, reconsider if you are presenting signs of ADHD.

6. You avoid or dislike tasks that call for sustained, mental effort. A common theme throughout this list is that the autonomy of adults can hide symptoms of ADHD. Because you are an adult, you can often avoid detail-oriented tasks without anyone really noticing. This means that you can avoid those tasks and not realize it's a problem. However, this can lead to problems, especially if you avoid paying your bills or performing other household responsibilities. If you have real trouble sitting down to pay your bills, this might be a hidden sign of ADHD.

7. You often lose items that are necessary or important for a task. Are you always losing your keys or your phone? Do you never know where you left your glasses? It's too easy to dismiss this symptom as a minor inconvenience, rather than what it is: A potential symptom of inattentive type ADHD.

8. You are easily distracted by intrusive thoughts. Because adults with undiagnosed ADHD have gone through their whole life without realizing they have a condition, you might just think that everyone's brain works like yours. The truth is most people do not get distracted by tangential thoughts. It's worth reflecting on your thought patterns and considering if you are showing signs of ADHD. An excellent strategy is to talk through your thought patterns with a friend or family member, to compare and contrast, and establish what is normal.

9. You are constantly forgetful. As adults live busy lives full of responsibilities, we often explain away short-term memory issues as the consequence of a high-paced, modern life. Have you ever arrived home with no memory of your drive from work? Have you ever entered a room and forgotten why you walked in? If you are constantly

experiencing this, you may be presenting a symptom of ADHD. It is important to realize that the forgetfulness associated with ADHD is not quite the same as impaired memory, however. You may find that your memory is excellent when you are directly attending to a task, but that you easily forget something routine or day-to-day. This is because ADHD impacts the attentiveness which is needed to form the memory in the first place, rather than impairing your ability to recover stored memories.

These hidden symptoms relate to inattentive type ADHD. However, it is also common for hyperactive/impulsive type symptoms to present differently in adults. This is because adults are more socialized than children and because adults with undiagnosed ADHD have generally learned to inhibit disruptive behaviors. After all, if you have not been able to inhibit those behaviors, this would probably have led to you being diagnosed with ADHD!

For example, restlessness is more likely to present as fidgeting in adults. Where a child might get up from their seat in class and run about, or start climbing the table, an adult will have learned to suppress this disruptive behavior so as not to get into conflict with others. As we have already mentioned earlier, a subtle sign of restlessness might be that you visit the bathroom more often, despite not actually needing the toilet. You may drink more water so you can get up to go to the watercooler more often.

If you are an adult with undiagnosed ADHD, it is almost an inevitability that your symptoms are hidden or subtler. That's why your ADHD is undiagnosed. The key is reflecting on your behaviors and thought patterns and teasing apart what is really going on. The good news is that you're already on the right track: If you're reading this book, you presumably suspect that you or a person you love is exhibiting symptoms of ADHD. This means you're already reflecting on your behaviors and scrutinizing your potential symptoms. If any of the symptoms above particularly resonate with you, it might be worth talking to a doctor about an appraisal.

It's also worth understanding that what is hidden from us can be more obvious to others. Even with all the self-reflection in the world, sometimes our patterns of behavior can be opaque to ourselves. Bilkey (2018) notes that a doctor should consider not only the patient's testimony but also the testimony of a patient's friends and family. Similarly, if you suspect that you are presenting symptoms of ADHD, it may be worth talking to someone close to you to see if they think the same. They may surprise you with what they say.

Ambiguities in ADHD

With all the misconceptions and subtleties that surround ADHD, it can be difficult to know if your behaviors amount to a likely case of the condition. The first thing to note is that this is okay: That's what your doctor is for. If you're not sure, it's a good idea to talk to your doctor. They will be able to arrange an appraisal that can help clarify your symptoms, potentially leading to a positive diagnosis. Putting this aside, however, it's also worth noting that a bit of ambiguity in your symptoms reflects the broad nature of ADHD as a condition. Braaten (n.d.) notes that "ADHD symptoms are something that exists on a spectrum or a continuum… ADHD isn't an all-or-nothing thing." If you're not sure if you have ADHD or not, it may be that you have a milder form of the condition.

Further complicating the matter is that the symptoms of ADHD can overlap with other common mental disorders. The intrusive thoughts of predominantly inattentive and combined type ADHD are easily confused with the racing thoughts of a general anxiety disorder. Trouble getting to sleep is associated not only with ADHD but also depression (and many other mental disorders). If that wasn't enough, many of these mental disorders are comorbid with ADHD, which means that someone with ADHD is more likely to have these other mental disorders than someone without ADHD. As a result, it can be difficult, or even impossible, to tease apart the symptoms of different disorders.

This is all to say that it's okay to be confused, and it's okay not to be sure. If you're reading this book, you probably already have enough suspicions about your own behaviors and thought patterns to make it worth talking to your doctor. You have nothing to lose by getting yourself appraised, apart from a little bit of your time. On the other hand, receiving treatment for newly diagnosed ADHD can be life-changing.

Healthy Habits

Once you have self-reflected, brought your suspicions to your doctor, and been diagnosed with ADHD, you might be wondering about the next step. Hopefully, your doctor has already outlined some sort of treatment plan, whether this involves medication or therapy designed to manage your symptoms. Either way, you'll find that managing your ADHD takes work and requires the knack of forming new habits. Even if you aren't diagnosed with ADHD, learning how to effectively form habits is a skill that can benefit anyone.

Milkman (2021) outlines five fundamental aspects of forming an effective habit. These are as follows:

1. Be specific in your goals. Do you make New Year's resolutions? An extremely common New Year resolution is to lose some weight—not only is it common as a resolution, but it is also common as a failed resolution. One of the problems is that it's not specific enough of a goal. Instead of aiming to generally lose weight, it's more effective to set a clear target: I want to lose ten pounds. Better yet, frame your goal around a specific activity: I want to stop eating outside of meals.

2. Support your goal with a detailed, cue-based plan. Let's continue with the example of wanting to lose some weight. Maybe you've decided on the specific goal of not eating outside of regular meals. It's now worth thinking about how to support that goal with a good plan. If you're currently in the habit of snacking just before lunch, it might be an idea to bring your lunch forward a little earlier in the day. Furthermore, Milkman (2021) notes that "an established, hyper-specific plan also forces you to anticipate and maneuver around obstacles."

3. Try to make your new habit fun. Sometimes this can be difficult: Especially if your new habit is about denying you something, like cutting down on your snacking. However, one thing you can do is take steps to gamify your new habit. This means building in rewards or a competitive element. If you're trying to lose weight and you really

enjoy going to the movies, why not say that you'll treat yourself to a cinema visit if you don't snack for a week?

4. Make your habit sustainable by building in flexibility. The more that your habit clashes with your daily routine, the harder it will be to sustain: As Milkman (2021) puts it, "if your routine becomes too brittle, you'll follow through less often." Continuing our example, sometimes you'll be working late. If you're starving, you should allow yourself the flexibility of a small, healthy snack to keep you going before you can get home. Otherwise, you'll end up binging or suffering some other setback that could have been avoided.

5. Find others to support you in your new habit. You are much more likely to stick to a new habit if you have social support. Just announcing your goal in a semi-public fashion can help hold you accountable, improving your chance of following through. If you want to stop snacking, announcing this on social media can be a quick, easy way of reinforcing your new habit. Furthermore, new habits are more likely to be successful if you form them with someone else. A lot of people want to cut down on their weight as a New Year's resolution. Why not consider having a "snack-free" buddy at work, so you can mutually support each other with the motivation and encouragement you need?

When it comes to ADHD, forming habits is going to be an integral part of managing your symptoms. Let's talk about diet, and about sleep hygiene. Most individuals with ADHD find that the severity of their symptoms is affected by what they eat and whether they're getting enough sleep. In both cases, habit forming is an essential part of managing your symptoms of ADHD.

Your Diet

Let's start with your diet. Kimball and Effiong (2021) note that the symptoms of ADHD can be improved by eating a balanced, nutritious diet. Interestingly, many children with ADHD also complain of constipation, suggesting a link between the condition and the food we are eating. Relatedly, the kinds of food that help relieve constipation have been evidenced to have a positive effect on attention levels. Kimball and Effiong suggest increasing your fiber and protein intake, whilst reducing simple carbohydrates like bread and sugar-rich foods. Instead of cereal for breakfast, why not consider a protein-rich egg? This can put you in the right mindset for the day, and also keep you feeling full for longer.

One of the differences between proteins and carbohydrates is in how they affect our insulin levels. Insulin is released by our body to break down sugars into energy that the body can use, and a hunger pang is typically associated with a crash in the amount of insulin in our blood. In the case of carbohydrates and other foods high in glucose (sugar), the pancreas floods the body with insulin to break down the food into energy, leading to a sudden boost in energy levels. This may give you short-term energy, but an insulin spike always leads to an insulin crash, where your energy levels plummet and you suddenly feel hungry. When it comes to proteins and other foods with less glucose, your body is less flooded with insulin, and the food takes longer to break down. This keeps your insulin levels stable and prevents the extremity of spikes and crashes that can affect your concentration, hunger levels, and mood.

Of course, a change of diet requires the forming of a new habit, especially if you are used to sugary snacks or eating a lot of carbohydrates. It can be difficult to form this new habit. Just remember the five elements of a successful habit: specificity, detail, fun, flexibility, and social support. With these elements in mind, let's consider what kind of habit you might want to adopt.

Because we want our new habit to be specific, your goal shouldn't be simply to eat fewer carbohydrates. We want something more specific than that. To start off with, maybe you can focus on one meal of the day and commit to replacing it with a protein-rich alternative. If you eat cereal for breakfast–especially if it is a sugar-rich cereal–you might set a specific goal to replace that cereal with porridge, an egg, or some other alternative that is protein-rich and lower in sugar. That goal is clear and precise, and you can hold yourself accountable with clear conditions of success and failure.

Now we think about the details. One of the advantages of cereal is that it's very quick to prepare: You just pour the cereal into a bowl, add milk, and enjoy. If you're shifting to porridge or a boiled egg, you'll need to give yourself a bit more time in the morning to accommodate making your breakfast. Think about your morning routine and whether you need to set your alarm clock a little earlier. If setting your alarm clock earlier would sacrifice much-needed sleep, you might need to think about going to bed a little earlier to keep your sleep at a healthy amount. Moreover, if you're shifting from cereal to another food, there are some mundane practicalities to consider. Do you have eggs? Chances are that you'll need to buy eggs more regularly to accommodate eating them more often. By getting ahead and planning for these practicalities, you're less likely to be caught out and break your new habit.

The third element of a successful habit is to make it as fun as possible. When it comes to having eggs and porridge for breakfast, a great strategy is to build variety into your meal. You can experiment with different berries and seasonings with your porridge, whilst chili powder can be a great option for giving your morning eggs a bit of a kick. Embrace your creativity and try new things. Even if they don't work, you can always try something different the next day: By engaging your creativity, you might find your new habit more enjoyable to maintain. If nothing else, if you find a recipe you love, the great taste of your new, protein-rich breakfast might be all the reward you need to keep your new habit going.

Next, let's think about how we can keep the habit flexible. The main thing is to give yourself a pass when you are just too short on time in the morning. Sometimes you can't avoid a late night: You may decide that your sleep is more important and prioritize getting a full eight hours instead of making porridge for breakfast. This is justifiable and valid. If that happens, give yourself the flexibility to eat something different for breakfast, even if that means a quick, sugar-rich cereal. On the other hand, maybe you can think about making up for the cereal with another meal that day. Instead of having a high-carb pizza or pasta dish for dinner, how about something with nuts or quinoa?

Finally, let's talk about social support for your new habit. If you live with someone else, an excellent way of supporting your new breakfast habit is to include the people you live with. For a start, if you commit to taking turns cooking breakfast for each other, you effectively halve the amount of effort your new habit will require. Cooking two eggs doesn't take much longer than cooking one, after all. Even if your partner doesn't want to join you in eating a protein-rich breakfast, their support and encouragement can be a great help when your morale is wavering. Maybe even just a poke to get you out of bed can prevent you from running out of time to cook.

Furthermore, the great thing about cutting down on carbs and other sugar-rich foods is that it won't just help with your ADHD symptoms. It'll also help you lose weight if you need to, and generally lower your risk of life-threatening conditions like diabetes and heart disease.

Your Sleep

Let's shift our focus to sleep hygiene. Kimball (& Effiong, 2021) goes so far as to say that "ADHD could be called a sleep disorder." Low (2021) agrees that getting enough sleep is a very important part of managing the symptoms of ADHD. But what is sleep hygiene? Does it just boil down to getting enough sleep? The answer is yes and no. Practicing good sleep hygiene aims at getting a healthy amount of sleep, but sleep hygiene is the method, rather than the goal.

An essential component of good sleep hygiene is consistency, which means you need to form the habit of going to bed and getting up at the same time every day. This means we need to form an effective habit with the five elements we've discussed. We need our goal to be specific. This means that you should try to commit to a specific time you'll go to bed, and a specific time you'll get up. Try to avoid vague terms like "earlier" and instead set a precise time. This will avoid any ambiguity and keep you accountable.

Now we come to the details. Depending on your schedule, fixing your sleep patterns may involve some planning. If you are really committing to your new habit, you'll maintain your sleep patterns not just over the week, but over the weekend as well. This might mean that you're up earlier on the weekends than you're used to and go to bed earlier as well. This might require you to shift some things around, to minimize any clash between your new, healthy habit and your current day-to-day life. However, remember that we want a new habit to be flexible. This means that your new sleep pattern shouldn't be a cudgel that gets in the way of a positive social life. It's okay to have a late night every so often to go on a date night or to spend some time with friends.

But we've skipped an important element of a good habit: Fun. When making a new habit of consistent sleep patterns, you may find it motivating to gamify your new schedule. Try to link maintaining your habit with rewards, tailoring those rewards to your own preferences. If you like tracking your progress on apps, consider wearing a cost-effective device like a Fitbit to measure your sleep patterns at night, and to chart how much of your sleep is REM or deep.

Finally, when thinking about sleep hygiene, getting the right social support can be crucial. This is because it's hard to stick to a sleep routine that puts you out of sync with everyone else in the household. If you live with a partner, ask if they would join you in keeping to a particular pattern of sleep. If necessary, it may be worth compromising to agree on a bedtime that suits everyone. Not only will this ensure that you're all functioning on the same schedule, but you'll also find it easier to get up in the morning if your partner is also awake and starting their day.

If you want to do more to practice good sleep hygiene, it's also worth thinking about your screen use around bedtime. All sleep experts advise that you should keep any screens outside the bedroom, including your mobile phone. This is because the blue light of such devices imitates daylight, which signals your brain to be more alert and active. This, of course, impacts your sleep. Many of us are guilty of this one but try to avoid scrolling through social media in your bed. Keep your phone out of the bedroom: If you need it for an alarm, it's worth investing in an affordable alarm clock instead. Ideally, your bed should be reserved for sleep and intimate moments with your partner. By restricting your time in bed to sleep you form a habit in your brain that should make it easier for you to fall asleep when you get into bed.

Thinking about your diet and sleep can have a huge impact on your life with ADHD and forming positive habits can be a great first step toward managing your symptoms. Furthermore, these are steps you can take today, regardless of your budget or lifestyle. However, it's always good to remember that you can form a habit one step at a time. Rome wasn't built in a day, and it's okay to start small and build up. If you're finding cooking breakfast to be particularly difficult, why not consider committing to making eggs on just Monday mornings to start with? As you build up the habit, it should get easier to stick to, allowing you to expand the habit to the rest of the week.

It's also worth considering how the forming of new habits will interact with symptoms of ADHD. In Chapter 6, we'll consider some specific strategies for maintaining a schedule and keeping up with time management: You may want to apply some of these strategies when forming the habits listed here. Distractibility, poor organization, and forgetfulness can make it tricky to form new habits, but there is help available. Just try your best, and don't be afraid to ask for help where you need it. The great thing is that these habits form a positive spiral. The more you keep to a nutritious diet and good sleep hygiene, the more you'll be able to manage your symptoms, which will in turn contribute to you maintaining your new habits.

Chapter 4:
Tackling Comorbidities

Antonio was diagnosed with ADHD as a child in the fifth grade. In many ways, he was a typical case: Exhibiting the hyperactivity that is so helpful in making a childhood diagnosis of ADHD hyperactive/impulsive or combined type. However, despite Antonio receiving treatment for his ADHD, he spent "years of his life [...] suffering from paralyzing anxiety that resulted in his missing classes, being housebound for days, and not being able to work" (Olivardia, 2022).

Eventually, Antonio's anxiety disorder was diagnosed when Antonio was in his last year of college. The trouble was, as Antonio himself puts it, "everyone assumed that my anxiety behaviors were just the hyperactivity part of my ADHD" (Olivardia, 2022). In fact, he had both ADHD and generalized anxiety disorder (GAD), occurring concurrently.

Corey was also diagnosed with ADHD as a child but found himself feeling anxious when he went to college: "Without the structure of high school and his parents' support, he felt lost" (Olivardia, 2022). He developed severe anxiety about writing papers and taking tests, which resulted in him sleeping poorly, which in turn left him feeling on edge throughout the day. He met the diagnostic criteria for GAD and, as Olivardia (2022) puts it, "needed treatment."

These two cases demonstrate two different problems people with ADHD can face when it comes to other, co-occurring mental disorders. In Antonio's case, he had GAD as well as ADHD. These conditions were comorbid, and neither had caused the other. However, because of overlapping symptoms in ADHD and GAD, Antonio's anxiety was masked, frustrating a proper diagnosis. The avoidance behaviors Antonio exhibited as part of his GAD were mistaken for symptoms of ADHD.

By contrast, Corey developed GAD as a consequence of his ADHD. When he was younger, Corey's symptoms of ADHD could be managed by the structure put in place by his parents and high school. However, at college, Corey no longer had this support to manage his ADHD. As his symptoms of ADHD worsened, Corey started to worry about his performance at college, which developed into an anxiety disorder.

There are two lessons to learn here. One: The symptoms of ADHD can mask the symptoms of other comorbid mental disorders. And two: The symptoms of ADHD can contribute to the development of another mental disorder.

Statistics for Comorbid Conditions

Unfortunately, many mental disorders are comorbid with ADHD. When we say that a mental disorder is comorbid with ADHD, we simply mean that if you have ADHD, you are more likely than someone without ADHD to also have one of these comorbid conditions. Bailey (2022) reports that people with ADHD are three times more likely to develop a mood disorder such as depression, adding that up to 70% of people with ADHD will be treated for depression at some point in their life. As we have seen with Antonio and Corey's stories, the reason for this comorbidity can vary. As both ADHD and depression are associated with dopamine dysregulation in the brain, it may be that both conditions share a common cause. On the other hand, sometimes depression can develop as a result of struggling with the symptoms of ADHD. Because ADHD can affect your academic and work performance, people with ADHD often suffer from low self-esteem. This negative self-appraisal can lead to the development of depression.

However, depression is not the only condition that is comorbid with ADHD. Bailey (2022) outlines some stark statistics:

- approximately 85% of adults with ADHD will be diagnosed with another mental disorder in their life

- 70% of people with ADHD will be treated for depression at some time in their life

- 50% of children with ADHD are impacted by learning disabilities, compared to 5% of children without ADHD

- 25-40% of adults with ADHD also have an anxiety disorder

- 40-80% of children with ADHD develop oppositional defiant disorder (ODD)

- 20-25% of adults with ADHD develop conduct disorder (CD)

- up to 20% of people with ADHD have bipolar disorder

- 60% of children diagnosed with either ADHD or sensory processing disorder (SPD) had both

- children with ADHD are 20 times more likely to exhibit symptoms of autism spectrum disorder

- 20-30% of adults with ADHD develop substance abuse problems at some time in their life

- 60-80% of children with Tourette's syndrome also have ADHD (this is one-directional: Less than 10% of children with ADHD have Tourette's syndrome)

When reading this list, you might be forgiven for feeling a little daunted. After all, living with and managing the symptoms of ADHD is challenging enough! However, it's worth remembering that these statistics are probabilistic. If you don't feel depressed, then it doesn't matter that 70% of people with ADHD are diagnosed with depression: You are not depressed. On the other hand, if you are dealing with the symptoms of another mental disorder, it's important not to ignore it. These statistics may seem dispiriting, but they are also a prompt for you to take your symptoms seriously. After all, you either have a comorbid condition or you don't. Once you are properly diagnosed, you can begin treating your conditions to manage your symptoms.

If your conditions are co-occurring, you may find that it is impossible to tease out the symptoms. Consider depression. A symptom of depression is having trouble motivating yourself to perform or finish tasks. Meanwhile, a symptom of ADHD is severe procrastination and difficulty following through on a project. You can appreciate how these symptoms overlap and may conceal each other. With this in mind, Montano (2014) notes that depression can mask ADHD. Relatedly, Bailey (2022) writes that it is sometimes difficult to separate symptoms of ADHD from symptoms of bipolar disorder: A manic episode may look a lot like hyperactivity, whilst a low state may present as a lack of motivation or severe inattentiveness.

Ultimately, if you are properly diagnosed, it doesn't really matter if it's not possible to map each symptom to a particular disorder. Happily, many treatments for these comorbid conditions are mutually supportive and compatible. The only thing to be worried about is whether your ADHD is masking a comorbid condition that you're not receiving treatment for. If you are in doubt, it's always worth considering the statistics above and talking to your doctor about your symptoms: Especially if you are finding that some of your symptoms are not being effectively managed by your ADHD treatment.

If your conditions are co-occurring, then the important thing is to get diagnosed and receive treatment. However, let's focus on cases where ADHD may contribute to the development of another mental disorder.

Practicing Self-Compassion and Positive Thinking

ADHD, especially if left untreated, can impact your academic performance, your career, and your relationships. This, in turn, can impact your self-esteem. Have you ever berated yourself for a supposed failure at work? Have you ever wondered why you can't just be normal? We all have these thoughts every now and again, but it's worth talking to someone if you're constantly putting yourself down, especially if your thoughts feel extreme. Low self-esteem can be a major contributor to the development of depression. Unfortunately, this creates a downward spiral: Developing depression will make it even harder for you to function at work or in relationships, which will contribute to your negative self-appraisals, which will further strengthen your depressive symptoms, and so on.

To combat this vicious cycle, it's worth thinking about practicing self-compassion. Think about it this way: If a loved one was struggling in their career, how would you help *them*? You wouldn't insult them or tell them that they weren't good enough because this would be cruel and counterproductive. However, if you accept that these methods are ineffective, why then would you use them against yourself?

We are often better to our friends than we are to ourselves. The first step is being cognizant of that discrepancy. Neff (n.d.) notes that it can be very effective to put your thoughts into writing: This forces you to think about what you are thinking, and to identify patterns in your behavior of thought. You can also use this as part of an exercise in self-compassion. Neff (n.d.) outlines the following exercise designed to foster self-care and self-compassion:

1. Write about a topic that makes you feel inadequate. As you do this, think about what emotions come up and make sure to include them in your writing.
2. Write a response to what you have just written from the perspective of an unconditionally loving friend. Try to infuse your response with acceptance, kindness, and caring.

3. After some time has passed, come back and read both letters again. Mark the differences in tone.

Let's consider this exercise in action. Suppose that you have recently suffered job loss, having found it difficult to organize yourself or follow through on projects. The first part of the exercise might look something like this:

> I am angry and hate myself for getting fired. I wish I was normal and wasn't such a failure. If I had been properly organized and wasn't so stupid, this wouldn't have happened.

Now consider what you might write from the perspective of a good friend. You might write something like the following:

> I'm sorry you lost your job; that must be really difficult for you. It's horrible that your ADHD has made your work so difficult but remember that your ADHD doesn't make you stupid or a failure. Maybe it's worth talking to your doctor about getting the help you need to manage your symptoms a little better. In the meantime, I promise that things will feel better after a little time has passed, and I love you for who you are.

As you have no doubt noticed, there is a stark difference in tone between the two passages. By writing down what we're thinking, our patterns of thought are put into black and white and become more obvious to ourselves. From there, we can start fostering self-compassion and self-care.

Many men balk at the idea of self-compassion, mistaking it for weakness or self-indulgence. This is a mistake. Practicing self-compassion is an important part of taking responsibility for your own mental health. Not only that, but it is a more effective way of managing your emotions and will lead to better outcomes. If you're not convinced, consider the successful tech entrepreneur and investor, Dan Martell. Every morning, he uses meditation to practice his attention skills, and practices positive journaling to put him in a better frame of mind (Martell, 2018).

A big part of many self-compassion exercises is the skill of reframing. This is about taking the time to think differently about a problem or event. We've seen an example of this in the exercise above, where we reframed losing your job in less blaming language. However, we can go further with our reframing.

Morin (2022) provides the following example: Suppose you were working for a promotion that involved a lot of travel, and you were unsuccessful. Your first impression may be to feel frustrated or upset at not getting the promotion. However, you can reframe the event by considering some potential downsides of that promotion. You would have had to travel a lot, which may have impacted your social relationships. You may have found it exhausting to be traveling so often, which might have impacted your sleep and your health. By reframing the event, you can think more positively about what's happened and avoid self-blame. Scott (2020) notes that reframing "can actually change your physical responses to stress because your body's stress response is triggered by *perceived* stress, more often than actual events."

Relatedly, Ackerman (2018) stresses the importance of fostering a growth mindset. A growth mindset requires you to recognize that you have the ability to grow and change what others may assume to be fixed or immutable characteristics. To understand this a little better, consider again the example of not getting the promotion you wanted. Someone with a fixed mindset may conclude that they do not have the skills to find promotion and that they may as well give up. By contrast, someone with a growth mindset knows that they have the ability to improve their chances of promotion the next time. They will consider how they went about seeking promotion and attempt to learn from the experience so they can succeed in the future. Fostering a growth mindset incorporates reframing and self-compassion because it turns negative events into opportunities for growth and encourages you to believe in your own ability to improve. Again, journaling can be very helpful in fostering a growth mindset: When something bad happens, write down your feelings from the perspective of a fixed mindset, and then write another passage from the perspective of a growth mindset. Then compare the two and reflect on the differences between them.

Let's continue the example of not getting that promotion. Writing from the perspective of a negative, fixed mindset, you might write the following:

> I didn't get the promotion because other people are better than me. I don't have the skills or ability to advance in this company, so I should stop trying for promotions: It's just a hurtful waste of time.

By contrast, you might write the following from a growth mindset perspective:

> This time, I didn't get the promotion. My boss suggested that they wanted more evidence of managing others, so I should work with my team leader to help manage some future projects. This will build on my leadership abilities and demonstrate to my boss that I have what it takes.

As you can see, a growth mindset is not only more positive, but it is more productive as well. It helps you avoid settling on global, negative impressions of yourself, which in turn can contribute to the development of depression and other mental orders.

Recognizing Disordered Thinking

The techniques we've discussed focus on self-compassion, with the goal of avoiding self-blame and negative self-esteem. In general, look out for the following examples of disordered, negative thinking (Mayo Clinic, n.d.):

- **filtering:** When you think about a situation, you filter out the positive aspects and focus on the negative aspects of that situation—did your boss really reprimand you, or did they offer two pieces of praise and one piece of constructive feedback?

- **personalizing:** Your first response to something bad happening is to blame yourself—did your friend cancel because they don't like you, or because they had to stay late at work?

- **catastrophizing:** You automatically anticipate the worst possible scenario—if you made a mistake at work, are you going to be fired, or will you just be asked to amend the error?

- **blaming:** You are quick to blame others for any bad thing that happens—are you late because of everyone else contributing to the traffic, or because you set off too late?

- **should-talk:** The opposite of blaming, you tend to assume that you are responsible for any bad thing that happens, and think in terms of what you "should" have done—if you fall ill, should you have taken more steps to protect yourself, or is it just something that happens sometimes?

- **magnifying:** You have a tendency to make a big deal out of relatively small problems—when you run out of milk, is your whole day ruined, or is it just a minor inconvenience?

- **perfectionism:** You hold yourself to an impossible standard and beat yourself up when you inevitably fall short—is making a mistake at work unforgivable, or is it just part of being human?

- **polarizing:** Also known as black-and-white thinking, you tend to see something as uniformly good or uniformly bad—did the person cut you off in traffic because they are a reprehensible human being, or because they were a little distracted?

These types of negative, disordered thinking can contribute to the development of GAD and depression. If you find yourself engaging in this kind of thinking, it's worth reflecting on that and thinking about how you could restate your feelings in a more positive way. This involves making use of self-compassion, reframing, and growth mindset techniques.

The Benefits of ADHD

Additionally, to prevent negative self-esteem, it's worth thinking about your strengths. You may be surprised to find that some of your strengths are related to your ADHD. Dan Martell (2018) goes so far as to describe his ADHD as a "superpower." Though this can be a psychologically healthy and motivational way of looking at your ADHD, it's also important to recognize that your symptoms need to be managed and properly harnessed to enjoy the benefits of ADHD.

For example, many people with ADHD, especially hyperactive/impulsive type and combined type ADHD find that they have higher energy levels than people without ADHD. This is supported by clinical evidence, with Sedgiwck et al. (2019) finding that all participants in their study described high energy levels as a positive aspect of their ADHD. Having high energy levels can make you more productive, as well as contribute to a healthier lifestyle with regular exercise. However, people with ADHD know that having a high energy level can be a double-edged sword. If not carefully managed and harnessed, your high energy can present as restlessness, fidgeting, or excessive talking. The key is focusing your energy on productive tasks and giving yourself an outlet for excess energy in the form of regular exercise or the occasional break. For example, in Chapter 2 we discussed the Pomodoro Technique: The practice of focusing for 25 minutes, breaking for 5 minutes, and then repeating three more times until a longer break. By getting up from your desk and walking around during your 5-minute break, you can burn off a little excess energy and keep yourself focused.

Another potential superpower of your ADHD is your ability to hyperfocus. Cherry (2021) notes that if you can harness and manage your hyperfocus, you can channel it into great bursts of productivity. Again, however, it's important to harness your hyperfocus productively. It's all a matter of context. Hyperfocus on a productive task can be extremely impressive and useful, but hyperfocus on a procrastinating activity can result in the day disappearing without much getting done. If you struggle with hyperfocus, consider carefully timing any breaks you take: The timer can help break your hyperfocus and get back to work.

Furthermore, studies show that people with ADHD tend to be more creative. This is probably a happy consequence of having intrusive thoughts: People with ADHD tend to link seemingly unconnected concepts more easily, leading to creative solutions to difficult problems. Abraham et al. (2006) found that children with ADHD displayed greater levels of creativity when being asked to perform certain tasks. Boot et al. (2017) replicated this result in adults with ADHD, but only when the adults were properly motivated with the opportunity to win a bonus for being more creative. Similarly, White and Shah (2011) found that adults with ADHD tended to be more creative than people without ADHD. Of course, this creative thinking can sometimes be an impediment when you are asked to perform a repetitive or tedious task, but it can be a huge boon in creative or problem-solving fields.

Similarly, you may think that impulsivity is a problem, but sometimes it is good to take risks. People with ADHD are less likely to dither: This can be tremendously important in life. Cherry (2021) adds that impulsivity can produce spontaneity and playfulness in relationships, which can strengthen those relationships and help you find profound joy. Additionally, Sedgwick et al. (2019) found that spontaneity plays a role in the development of courage. The important thing is to harness your impulsivity for those contexts where it will be helpful and to take a second breath where it's needed. Sometimes it can be helpful to talk to a friend or your partner before making a decision, so you can get another point of view and decide whether your impulsivity is advantageous or harmful in the context.

There is also evidence to suggest that people with ADHD do well in a crisis. adda (n.d.) reports that ADHD brains often produce more theta waves than other brains, which is indicative of a state of deep relaxation. This is reflected in the fact that people with ADHD are overrepresented in crisis fields such as doctors, police officers, and other emergency services.

Finally, like many people with mental health conditions, people with ADHD tend to demonstrate increased resilience, empathy, and self-awareness. Because you have struggled with your symptoms your entire life, you have naturally fostered your reliance, and you have an understanding that other people may be struggling as well. Chan et al. (2021) found that parents and teachers rate most children with ADHD as resilient. Furthermore, because you have learned to self-assess your behaviors, identify triggers, and carefully manage your symptoms, you are inevitably going to be more self-aware than most.

These advantages of ADHD are real and are to be celebrated. As Duane Gordon, a computer consultant with ADHD, puts it: "I always see the weirdness in the world, and I appreciate it [...] I can hyper-focus and be extremely productive when I'm passionate about something. I'm also extremely effective in emergency situations. When most people panic, I actually become calmer" (Booth, 2018).

With that in mind, when you're next tempted to put yourself down, consider your strengths as well as your weaknesses. Symptoms of ADHD can be difficult to manage and can cause problems in your work and relationships, but they can also be harnessed to your advantage. You may be impulsive, but you don't dither. You may be distractible, but you can connect concepts that others can't. You may be prone to procrastination, but when you focus on a task, you can be amazingly productive. Think about your abilities and your unique capabilities and try to avoid thoughts that put you down or lower your self-esteem. This will help you avoid the development of depression, GAD, and other disorders.

If you're still not convinced, consider the many celebrities who say they have ADHD (Nall 2021):

- the musicians Adam Levine, Dave Grohl, Justine Timberlake, and Solange Knowles

- the actors Channing Tatum and Zooey Deschanel

- the athletes and professional dancers Karina Smirnoff, Michael Phelps, Shane Victorino, Simone Biles, Terry Bradshaw, and Tim Howard

- the businessmen Richard Branson and Dan Martell

- the senator Scott Kelly

Each one of them is living proof that having ADHD doesn't make you stupid or destined for failure.

Harmful Coping Strategies

We've focused on depression and GAD because these tend to be the mental health conditions that follow ADHD, rather than occur concurrently. Another thing to consider is that people with ADHD are at a much greater risk of obesity. Weissenberger et al. (2017) suggest that this may be because people with ADHD are self-medicating with food to help cope with stress and frustration. Relatedly, people with ADHD are more likely to smoke—again, this may be an attempt at self-medication because nicotine affects your dopamine levels in the brain, which are adversely affected by ADHD. However, if you smoke, you are more likely to misuse drugs and alcohol. In particular, hyperactive/impulsive type ADHD is associated with substance abuse, which can have a profoundly negative impact on your work and relationships.

The key thing is to make sure you are being effectively treated for your ADHD. Effective treatment can help you manage your symptoms and avoid needing to self-medicate with harmful habits. Furthermore, be assured that there is no positive correlation between taking ADHD medication and substance misuse. AADD-UK (n.d.) notes that the reverse is actually true: Your risk of substance abuse dramatically falls if your ADHD is diagnosed and is being treated. This is because you are getting the help you need, and you do not need to self-medicate with alcohol or illicit drugs.

You have been living with ADHD your entire life. This means that you have at least an implicit understanding of how to manage your symptoms. If you are receiving proper treatment and medication, you may be in the position to harness your ADHD and achieve some incredible results. Remember that "ADHD thrives on a lack of structure," (Finch 2017), and builds a self-aware routine that makes the most of your abilities. For example, if you know that you are prone to hyperfocus in the morning, consider scheduling your most important tasks for the morning: You might be able to dramatically increase your daily productivity as a result.

Matt Curry, the founder of The Hybrid Shop, was diagnosed with ADHD in 1978 in the seventh grade. He manages his ADHD without medication and harnesses his symptoms to his advantage. Every morning, he channels his energy and creativity by writing down all of his ideas on a whiteboard. From there, he picks out the three best ideas on the whiteboard and breaks them into three parts: what he wants to do, how he will do it, and why he will do it. Of course, sometimes Matt's symptoms can set his mind racing. When he needs to slow down his thoughts, he goes for a walk or a drive, or practices meditation. However, Matt notes that his energy and hyperfocus have translated to success: "ADHD is my superpower. I'm successful because of it, not in spite of it" (Bailey, 2020). He encourages everyone with ADHD to find their niche: "Put yourself in situations where you are going to be successful. People with ADHD are good at sales. You might be good at social work or other jobs where you are helping people. Use your strengths to find your own path in life" (Bailey, 2020).

You have your own strengths. They may even originate from your ADHD. Recognize those strengths, and utilize them for a happier, more fulfilling life.

A Brief Intermission

At this point, I'd like to thank you for reading this book. I know that many people with ADHD can struggle with the sustained mental effort of reading, and it means a great deal to me that you have devoted your time and energy to my work.

If you have enjoyed the book so far, I would be delighted if you would rate and review it. Honest feedback helps other potential readers find the book and helps me improve my craft. It really makes a big difference, and it will only take you a minute.

You have the power!

Chapter 5:
ADHD and Men

Bill didn't know he had ADHD until his wife, Cheryl, asked him to read a book that her therapist had recommended. When he started reading, Bill only made it fifty pages before he burst into tears: "It laid out every story from our marriage" (Orlov, 2017).

For a long time, Bill and Cheryl's marriage had been struggling. It had gotten so bad that Cheryl was actually planning to divorce Bill after their child had left home. When she talked about her husband to her therapist, the therapist suggested that Bill might have ADHD. Bill had real problems with his short-term memory and would often seem forgetful and distracted. Cheryl couldn't trust him to follow through with a task and thought she just had to "scream louder" to be heard (Orlov, 2017). Meanwhile, Bill was "flailing in the water" (Orlov, 2017). In response to his wife's mounting frustration, he would retreat into himself, his self-confidence shattered.

When Bill was diagnosed with ADHD, the situation changed. They could now work together on managing Bill's symptoms, and they started to repair their marriage. Bill now realizes that his ADHD was making Cheryl feel "unsafe and unheard" (Orlov, 2017). Because he had lived with ADHD his entire life, Bill had always been comfortable with chaos: Now, he realizes that this chaos has a profound impact on the other people in his life and leaves his wife feeling insecure and unmoored. For her part, Cheryl now recognizes that Bill's symptoms are not a form of passive aggressiveness or maliciousness, but symptoms of a mental health condition. Now that they are working together, they've come to appreciate each other for who they are. As Cheryl puts it: "I love being married to someone who believes that the world is a myriad of opportunities" (Orlov, 2017).

Bill and Cheryl's story may seem familiar to many men with ADHD, especially if you were diagnosed later in your life and your relationship. When ADHD is undiagnosed, symptoms like forgetfulness and distractibility are too easily misinterpreted by your significant other as callousness or carelessness. Because your partner doesn't understand that your behavior is symptomatic of a treatable mental disorder, they can't help but take your behavior personally. Like in Bill and Cheryl's case, your partner may feel hurt and frustrated, and take it out on you in the form of shouting and nagging. This can lead you to withdraw further from your partner and retreat into yourself: An understandable coping strategy, but one that will ultimately weaken your relationship further. Unfortunately, these difficulties are borne out by statistics. Montano (2014) reports that the rates of divorce are doubled for people with ADHD.

However, like with Bill and Cheryl, the situation is far from hopeless. ADHD is treatable and often, simply awareness of the condition can have a restorative effect on a relationship affected by ADHD. It's very important for your significant other to be able to realize that your behaviors are not aimed at them, or in any way indicative of your feelings for them. For your part, when you are diagnosed with ADHD, you can learn to communicate better and manage your symptoms.

As Hovde (2022) reports, men are more likely than women to be diagnosed with hyperactive/impulsive and combined type ADHD. However, hyperactive and impulsive symptoms of ADHD present very differently in adult men than in boys. Hinojosa (2022) notes that "men don't typically exhibit intense symptoms of hyperactivity/inattentiveness. However, they experience difficulty with mood regulation, developing healthy sleep routines, heightened procrastination, and a decreased tolerance for frustrations." Where boys may run around a classroom or start climbing the desk, adult men have learned that these behaviors are disruptive. Instead, their hyperactivity and impulsivity are channeled into fidgeting and emotional dysregulation. In particular, men with ADHD often present "frequent emotional dysregulation, touchiness with criticism or conflict, and/or avoidance behaviors around conflict or emotions" (Hinojosa, 2022). Sometimes, ADHD can be misdiagnosed as an anger management problem, because men with ADHD have a hard time keeping their frustrations in check.

These symptoms can be very challenging to a relationship. Men with ADHD tend to be more forgetful, forcing their partners to repeat themselves. Because men with ADHD have trouble with distractions and following through on a task, their partners can feel let down by their behaviors. This leads to mounting frustration that inevitably results in conflict between men and their partners. Furthermore, because ADHD also contributes to emotional dysregulation, this conflict is more likely to be charged and hurtful. Men with ADHD learn to avoid conflict by lying or withdrawing into themselves, but this can result in a breakdown of trust and mutual love.

You may recognize some of these behaviors in yourself. Do you often feel irritable and unable to keep your frustrations in check? Have you learned to close yourself off to avoid painful encounters? In Chapter 1, we talked about how conflict can be painful and uncomfortable. Orlov (2022) notes that men often have more difficulty than women in recovering from a conflict: Research suggests that men's blood pressure remains elevated for longer and that men have more difficulty calming themselves down. Because elevated blood pressure is physically uncomfortable, it is no surprise that men learn to avoid the feeling: To avoid the conflict in the first place by distancing themselves from their partner.

Managing Your Symptoms in a Relationship

The important thing is not to resist an ADHD diagnosis. As Orlov (2022) writes, being diagnosed with ADHD is not the same as accepting blame for a relationship that is affected by the condition. Generally, it's best to avoid all talk of blame whatsoever. Blame puts you and your partner on different sides of a conflict, when, in truth, you want to be working together on rebuilding your relationship. Your responsibility is to be honest to yourself and your partner and to take steps to recognize your patterns of behavior and manage your symptoms of ADHD. Meanwhile, your partner must learn not to take your symptomatic behaviors personally, and to engage with you productively and lovingly. Orlov (2022) suggests eight positive ways that a partner can communicate with a man with ADHD:

1. When starting a conversation, use a soft opener instead of being blunt.
2. Before continuing with your conversation, wait until your man has transitioned his focus to you.
3. Though you may feel angry, try to remain calm and respectful.
4. To avoid blame and unhelpful conflict, use "I" statements instead of "you" statements—instead of "you should pay more attention to me," you might instead say "sometimes I feel like I'm not being listened to, and that makes me feel hurt."
5. More generally, try to avoid critiquing or parenting your man.
6. Consciously decide to not add to your man's shame.
7. Make use of physical touch as much as possible.
8. Try to find humor in the situation and recognize the positive aspects of your lives together.

Meanwhile, if you are a man with ADHD, it's worth thinking about how your symptomatic behaviors can be challenging to your partner. Your empathy can go a long way, especially if you communicate that empathy to your partner. Ultimately, your partner may think that they don't matter to you. By taking the time to understand their feelings, and communicating that to them, you can let them know that they do matter to you and that you are trying your best. This can make all the difference.

It's also important to have a sense of humor about yourself. Humor is a great way to diffuse tension and avoid conflict in a more positive, joyful way. If you can learn to laugh with your partner about your forgetfulness or distractibility, this can help ease frustrations and keep your relationship joyful and loving. On the other hand, it's okay to feel self-conscious about your symptoms: If you don't find it funny, it's healthy to communicate this to your partner. Just try to communicate clearly and calmly, and remember that your partner is just trying to channel their frustrations into a more positive outlet.

Meanwhile, it's worth accepting your self-defense mechanisms for what they are. There is no need to assign blame or guilt: You have been living with ADHD your entire life, potentially undiagnosed and untreated, and it is understandable that you have put in place coping strategies to help you function. It is a testament to your resilience and strength that you have come this far without help. Now, however, it is time to recognize that withdrawing into yourself will undermine the trust of your relationship. If you keep distancing yourself from your significant other, that distance may result in the relationship coming to an end.

Getting in Touch With Your Emotions

Society does not put much focus on teaching boys and men to express their emotions. This can be very damaging to young men, especially young men with ADHD because relationships thrive when there is open and honest communication. Orlov (2022) suggests that it's worth taking time to routinely assess how you are feeling. A good strategy is to set reminders to think about your current mood and emotions: Like riding a bike, after a bit of practice, it will become second nature. Furthermore, when you're thinking about your current mood—especially if it is negative—try to identify what triggered your current emotions.

By taking the time to reflect and assess yourself, you can process your feelings healthily and with a little bit of distance. Try it now! How do you feel? If your mind goes blank when you think about these kinds of questions, you may find it helpful to identify a few of the emotions listed below (provided by Christina, n.d.):

- energetic

- grateful

- creative

- happy

- loved

- calm

- sad

- tired

- cranky

- alone

- jealous

- frustrated

- disappointed

- anxious

- lost

Feel free to add your own: This is far from an exhaustive list but is designed to help get your self-reflection juices going. In addition, I've included some feelings below that are often experienced by people with ADHD:

- restless

- distractible

- focused

- defensive

- impatient

- driven

- withdrawn

- bored

- hyper

When you've identified how you're currently feeling, now think about what has triggered you feeling this way. Depending on the situation, some triggers may be easier to identify than others. For example, you might feel cranky because you've just experienced some setback. Others might be a little harder to identify. If you feel anxious and don't know why, think about what has recently happened and see if you can determine a trigger for how you're feeling. It is okay if this takes a little time, or even if you're not sure. This is a skill: The more you practice, the better you will get at it.

Relatedly, you might find it helpful to make a record of your self-reflections in a journal or on an app like Mood Log. By making a record of your feelings and their triggers, you can start to identify patterns that might not be obvious on any given occasion. For example, maybe you start to realize that you feel distractible and restless just before your lunch break. This might be a sign that you have excess energy from sitting at your desk for too long. The more you can be aware of your triggers and patterns of behavior, the better you can manage your symptoms.

It's also worth including your partner. Orlov (2022) notes that it is very helpful for partners to encourage men with ADHD to practice talking about their own emotions. Because men with ADHD have often learned avoidance behaviors (and, as a man, has probably not been encouraged to talk about their emotions when they were growing up), a bit of prompting, encouragement, and support can make all the difference. If you are a man with ADHD, consider asking for your partner's help. They should be happy to help you talk about your feelings, and this will build trust and love in your relationship.

When it comes to relationships and ADHD, it's also worth knowing that ADHD is comorbid with rejection sensitive dysphoria (RSD). Hovde (2022) notes that RSD is typified by an extreme sensitivity to rejection. In men, this may present as anger, sarcasm, defensiveness, seeming insensitive, apathy, needing to be right, or self-centeredness. Essentially, these are symptoms of RSD because they are attempts to emotionally protect yourself from rejection or the possibility of rejection. Bonior (2019) expands on the condition further:

> People with RSD have such a strong emotional reaction to negative judgments, exclusion, or criticism from others that it sends them into a mental tailspin, leading to rumination and the

pit-of-the-stomach malaise that won't let them move forward with their day. They feel like failures, disproportionate to what has actually occurred. They may feel rage and want to lash out. They often exaggerate how people are against them, how much people dislike them, or they carry long-term shame (para. 5).

If this describes you, then you may have RSD that is untreated. Currently, RSD is not recognized in the DSM-5 as a mental health condition, but it is getting increasing attention, especially for its association with ADHD. In many cases, the treatment you are receiving for your ADHD may help manage symptoms of RSD. In addition, cognitive behavioral therapy (CBT) techniques can be an effective way of managing RSD.

Because RSD can be so harmful to your relationships, it's worth taking the condition seriously and talking to your doctor if you show symptoms. Though you are unlikely to be formally diagnosed, your doctor can still refer you to a therapist who can help you with the condition, especially if you have already been diagnosed with ADHD.

Honing Your Social Skills

Unfortunately, ADHD can lead to a downward spiral when it comes to improving our social skills in childhood. Like with many things in life, the more practice you have with social interactions, the better you'll be with them. However, because symptoms of ADHD can make those social interactions difficult, children with ADHD often have less opportunity to practice their social skills. As CHADD (n.d.-b) puts it, people with ADHD can "exhibit behavior that is often seen as impulsive, disorganized, aggressive, overly sensitive, intense, emotional, or disruptive." This can lead to children with ADHD being rejected or shunned by their peers. This, in turn, means that children with ADHD have fewer opportunities to learn about appropriate social interaction. This can then lead to problems that extend into adulthood.

If you feel like you've never quite mastered social interaction, the first thing to realize is that it is okay. The fact that you are reading this book demonstrates that you are determined and on the path to self-improvement and change. CHADD (n.d.-b) offers the following handy tips and advice to help you hone your social skills:

- **Increase your likeability:** Certain characteristics make us more likable than others. Consciously commit to fostering these traits. They include kindness, sincerity, understanding, trustworthiness, dependability, humor, cheerfulness, responsibility, friendliness, warmth, intelligence, honesty, thoughtfulness, selflessness, trustfulness, consideration, loyalty, reliability, and happiness.

- **Visualization:** When you can anticipate a given social interaction, it can be helpful to mentally rehearse it in your head beforehand.

- **Attitude:** Be open to feedback, even if it is negative, and welcome the idea that your social skills can and will improve with effort.

- **Observe others:** Pay attention to how other people behave in typical social interactions.

- **Prompts:** Make use of prompts to help you stay focused and quiet. You might wear a vibrating watch that prompts you to wait your turn in conversations, or you might work with your friends or partner on the use of a specific gesture.

- **Roleplay:** Practicing social interaction with a therapist, friend, family member, or partner is an effective way of improving your skills.

- **Knowledge:** Reading more about the skills of social interaction can familiarize you with the skills you want to cultivate.

- **The echo:** Get in the habit of summarizing what someone just said to you, so you check in with them and avoid potential misunderstandings. It will also demonstrate to the person you're talking to that you're listening.

- **Goals:** Don't try to do everything at once. Work on one element of social skills at a time.

Social skills are like any other kind of skill: With practice, training, and study, you can improve upon them.

It's also important for men with ADHD to think about the subtext of a conversation and to pay attention to subtle conversational cues. These cues are often difficult to spot, but they give clues about the way you're expected to behave in that context. CHADD (n.d.-b) offers the following advice. When trying to identify subtext, it's important to pay attention to a person's particular choice of words, as well as their body language, behavior, tone of voice, and their eyes. For example, if someone says, "I'll do it *if you want*," this probably means that they don't really want to do it. On the other hand, if they say, "I'd love to do it," they are probably sincere. Meanwhile, an open posture and an enthusiastic tone of voice suggest positivity and friendliness, while a more guarded posture indicates that the individual is closed-off or defensive. Relatedly, remember that polite behavior can often disguise someone's actual feelings. With this in mind, learn to identify when someone is "just being polite," so that you aren't led into misunderstandings. For example, most people will default to being polite when you are meeting them for the first time.

Furthermore, it's worth paying closer attention to someone's actions than their words. People often say one thing and do another. As the old adage goes, actions speak louder. If your partner says that everything is fine, but seems to be avoiding eye contact, just generally avoiding you, or simply acting strangely, it's likely that something is wrong.

When it comes to specific contexts, it is helpful to pay attention to what other people are doing. This means paying attention to how other people are dressed, whether they are sitting or standing, and so on. You can take these as cues to your own behavior, to make sure that you don't act inappropriately in the situation. If everyone is formally dressed, for example, you will want to act more formally. If everyone is sitting down, it may be considered disruptive behavior to wander about the room. Additionally, if you can, find a guide who can help you navigate these kinds of situations. More generally, a guide to help you find subtext will help you avoid inappropriate behavior and get better at spotting social cues on your own.

Finally, though the symptoms of ADHD will sometimes make it difficult, try to remain focused. Unfortunately, just a momentary lapse can lead to misunderstanding. You can mitigate this somewhat by the use of the echo (see above), but it's good to stay present and attentive. On the other hand, don't be too hard on yourself: You're trying. That's more than can be said for many.

Men With ADHD in the Workplace

We've discussed the ways that ADHD can affect men with their relationships, but it's also important to discuss how ADHD can affect men in their careers. Orlov (2022) notes that "many men define themselves in large part by their work," which can lead to severe emotional distress when ADHD impacts your working life. Because men with ADHD tend to be more impulsive and distractible, they are more likely to be disciplined or fired or to quit their jobs themselves out of boredom or hostility towards their workplace. Furthermore, all the relationship difficulties that come from symptoms of ADHD apply equally to your relationships with your co-workers. This can put additional stress on your working life and lead to dysfunction in the office.

Orlov (2022) writes that "many men report working longer hours than their co-workers to manage the workload and stay organized." Because men are often raised to base their self-esteem on their job performance and career, work problems related to ADHD can put tremendous pressure on men. As we saw in Chapter 4, this pressure can impact your self-esteem and even contribute to the development of other mental health disorders such as generalized anxiety disorder and depression.

In Chapter 6, we will discuss ways of organizing yourself that can help you manage your symptoms of ADHD and stay on top of your work. In the meantime, remember that your employer is legally obligated to make reasonable adjustments for you if your work is severely affected by your ADHD. This is because of the Americans with Disabilities Act (ADA), which seeks to protect people with physical and mental disabilities from discrimination in the workplace.

As we have seen repeatedly in this book, the first step is to understand your patterns of behavior. If you can't get anything done because your phone keeps ringing and breaking your focus, it may be worth talking to your employer about setting your phone up, so it goes straight to voicemail. You can then schedule a time in your day to go through your messages. If you find that background chatter makes it impossible to concentrate, your employer may agree that you can listen to music or white noise on headphones while you're at your desk. Similarly, if you are constantly feeling restless, it can be helpful to talk with your employer so that they understand that using a stress ball or fidget spinner is not disruptive, but helpful to your work and productivity.

Bringing things back to your relationships, it's also important to recognize that everything bleeds into each other. Difficulties at work—especially if you find yourself working longer hours to compensate—can lead to difficulties at home.

For example, Orlov (2022) notes that it can be particularly difficult for men with ADHD to find a new job if they do suffer job loss. Unfortunately, the skills and abilities needed for job hunting are often incompatible with the skillset of an individual with ADHD. Job hunting requires sustained effort, planning, and a tolerance for rejection: All aspects of life that many people with ADHD find challenging. Orlov (2022) writes that this can sometimes lead to avoidance behaviors, with some men refusing to look for a job instead of tackling how they feel: "Fear and stress represent weakness to many men; stubborn feels strong, even if it isn't in a person's best interest."

Of course, there is nothing weak about processing your emotions healthily. If you're someone who tends to bottle up how you feel, you may be holding yourself back and weakening your resilience. By being honest to yourself and others, and being your authentic self, you can become emotionally stronger and manage your symptoms of ADHD a little better.

The Neurodiversity of Our World

Ultimately, we are all different. Genius Within (n.d.) reports that 7% of the population have mental health needs: Almost one in ten people. Increasingly, our society is opening up to the idea of neurodiversity. Genius Within (n.d.) offers some further, eye-opening statistics about the reality of neurodiversity in our world:

- 90% of disabilities are invisible, meaning they are not immediately apparent to a casual observer

- 1-2% of people are autistic

- 10% of people are dyslexic

- 5% of people are dyspraxic

- 1-2% of people have Tourette's syndrome

- 5% of people have an acquired brain injury

Neurodiversity is an undeniable fact about our species, and, more recently, society is waking up to that reality. Neurodiversity is a good thing because society functions better when populations have a range of skills. For example, people with ADHD are often creative and entrepreneurial, whilst people with autism are disproportionately represented in scientific fields. As society becomes more informed and tolerant of neurodiversity, we have the opportunity to organize ourselves by our strengths and by our interests, for the betterment of all.

Just as there is neurodiversity in the general population, there is considerable diversity within individual groups. If you have ADHD but don't feel particularly entrepreneurial, that's more than okay. Remember that ADHD incorporates a large range of symptoms. If you are deeply passionate about financial systems and possess hyperfocus, you may excel in accounting with ADHD, even though that might not be the typical career path for someone with an attention disorder. The important thing is to try and understand each other a little better and to celebrate our strengths that, more than often, can compensate for each other's weaknesses. Brian Scudamore, founder, and CEO of O2E and 1-800-GOT-JUNK credits his success to his ability to find people who can compensate for his own shortcomings. While Brian handles the vision for his companies, he works closely with his COO to manage the day-to-day details (Bailey, 2022).

This greater understanding of neurodiversity and our differing talents is also very important in relationships. Cook and Stephanie have been married for 45 years, but, for much of their long marriage, they were struggling (Orlov, 2017). Cook had undiagnosed ADHD, and was often agitated, impulsive, or suffered from short-term memory loss. Stephanie couldn't predict how he would act on a day-to-day basis. She didn't understand why he would suddenly have to get out of the house and interpreted Cook's alternative way of doing things as deliberate sabotage and passive aggression. In Stephanie's case, her frustration boiled over into rage, but the angrier she was, the more Cook withdrew: And he was quiet, to begin with. Stephanie started to hate herself for what she was becoming. Their marriage was on the rocks.

With a late diagnosis of ADHD and a bit of understanding, Cook and Stephanie have been able to turn things around. Cook speaks of a sense of "calmness" (Orlov, 2017) now that he understands more about the behaviors he is trying to control. To help deal with his short-term memory problems, Cook uses a whiteboard to jot down reminders about daily tasks. Meanwhile, Stephanie now understands Cook's condition and can help him manage his symptoms in a more productive and loving way. As Cook puts it, they have made "great strides" (Orlov, 2017). They have learned that their marriage is resilient and can overcome any obstacle.

The key to all these stories is the understanding that comes from open and honest communication. Communicating your feelings helps your partner understand that you do care and love them, and builds the kind of trust that contributes to lifelong relationships. Though this is especially important for men with ADHD, due to the pressures their symptoms can put on a relationship, ultimately it is good advice for everyone: Be open, be trusting, be receptive, and be empathetic. That's how good relationships last.

Chapter 6:
Directing Your Executive Function

Susan Baroncini-Moe, executive coach and author of *Business in Blue Jeans* (2013), was diagnosed with ADHD in her late 30s. For years, she had experienced difficulty completing projects, forgot small details frequently, and tended to talk a lot. Her diagnosis made everything make sense, offering a previously elusive self-understanding that is very common to people who are diagnosed with ADHD in their adulthood.

To manage her symptoms and improve her executive functions, Susan hired a coach to hold her accountable for her goals and to remind her of her accomplishments to boost her motivation. Knowing that she had to put in place strategies to improve her organization, she created organizational systems to help her and managed her restlessness by working at a treadmill desk, exercising regularly, and practicing meditation. Despite her struggles, Susan is proud of who she is: "I realized it really didn't matter whether ADHD was responsible for my quirkiness [...] I am who I am. I have ADHD. And that's just how it is" (Bailey, 2022).

Peterson (2019) explains that our executive functions are the functions of the brain responsible for inhibition, attention, memory, processing speed, and planning. If you have ADHD, you are probably intuitively familiar with executive functions: They are the functions that you tend to have trouble with! Put into one word, executive functions are about organization. The executive functions are associated with the prefrontal areas of the brain. Kim et al. (2010) have found that the ADHD brain has a reduced blood flow to some of the prefrontal areas of the brain, which goes some way to explain why executive functions are impaired.

The good news is that we can boost and support our executive functions by putting into place useful habits. If you have ADHD, it's likely that you've already adopted habits to support your organization. This might be as simple as having a to-do list, or more involved with an implicit system for decluttering your space. This chapter will add to these habits and provide some useful tips for further boosting your executive functions.

Using Apps to Manage Your ADHD

Many people with ADHD note that they find apps particularly helpful in managing their symptoms. As we all know, apps are ubiquitous in our day and age, and if you can think of something an app might do, there probably already exists an app that does just that.

Ferguson (2021) uses apps to aid his organization and time management, like Trello or Todoist to plan out his day and provide an easily referenced to-do list. Finch (2017) also recommends Todoist. The app includes a scheduler and a priority feature, so you can order tasks you need to complete in terms of importance or time sensitivity. It is also highly customizable, which means you can tailor your use of the app to best help you. For example, Finch (2017) splits different elements of his life across different tabs on the app, keeping everything organized. Another key feature of Todoist is its smart scheduling feature: The app tracks your productivity habits and uses that information to recommend which days and times are best for you to perform certain tasks. This gives you extra help in learning about your patterns of behavior, which we know is key to managing your symptoms.

Another useful app for people with ADHD is Grid Diary, which can be used as an effective tool for fostering self-awareness and an understanding of your symptoms. Grid Diary is a journal app that splits different aspects of your life (such as work and family) into a grid. You'll be surprised with how effective this can be as a prompt, helping you to open up and be more aware of your feelings and triggers. Like Todoist, Grid Diary is also highly customizable. You can change the title of each grid to reflect the different areas of your life, or use their suggestions to prompt journaling with specific questions like "How did I sleep last night?" or "What am I most grateful for today?"

Meanwhile, if you're struggling with email inbox clutter, don't worry: There's an app for that. Finch (2017) recommends the Chuck app. Chuck sorts through your emails in a systematized fashion, avoiding the need to manually click through every email to decide what you want to do with it. For example, Chuck sorts your emails by sender, time, or subject, so it can be used to mass archive emails that are over a year old, or from senders that aren't relevant to your life, such as email newsletters you accidentally subscribed to. Finch (2017) notes that he used the Chuck app to archive over 100,000 of his own emails in less than an hour. The only downside is that Chuck is only available on Apple processing systems.

There are many more apps available. If you don't feel confident with new apps, using old favorites like Google Calendar can help you schedule your day and stay organized. Furthermore, many of these functions can be replaced with pen and paper journaling, according to your preference. When it comes to these techniques and aids, the most important thing is sticking to their use. In particular, a to-do list or day planner is most effective when you have fostered the habit of using it. At the start, try to commit to looking at your day planner at least three times a day: At the start of your day, at lunch, and in the early evening. You want to build the habit of using your organizational tools until it becomes second nature to do so. Apps offer another advantage on this front: You can set reminders and notifications to remind you to check apps and stay on top of what you need to do in a day.

Dealing With Clutter and Mess

Let's move away from apps and talk about clutter. A cluttered space—whether this is virtual, such as your email inbox, or physical, such as your desk—can be distracting. If you have too much clutter in your space, it will be harder to maintain focus and attention on what you should be doing. Furthermore, you may start losing track of things: Losing them to the clutter exacerbates problems of forgetfulness. Though everyone can benefit from clearing their clutter, people with ADHD especially benefit from decluttering and having a distraction-free workspace.

Unfortunately, decluttering is a task that is not well-suited to the typical mind of someone with ADHD. It involves organization and sustained mental effort, and it can be hard to be passionate about tidying up. With that in mind, the websites CHADD (n.d.-a) and Advanced Psychiatry Associates (2021) offer practical advice for decluttering your space if you have ADHD. Their advice is broadly similar and summarized below. The basic principle is to break down a bigger task into a series of smaller tasks, to make it feel more manageable and to avoid procrastinating.

1. Break down your space into areas, either by function or location. For example, if you're looking to declutter your home, you might break down the space into rooms. If you're working on organizing your desk, you might split your space into your stationary section, your computer section, and where you keep your paperwork and files. Other ways of breaking down the space involve quartering—using imaginary lines that cut horizontally and vertically to split a space into four sections—or dividing the space like a clock, with each number from 1-12 of a clock being an area of the space.

2. For each of these areas, try to estimate how long it will take to declutter that area. As you're doing this, it can be helpful to rank the areas by how easy they will be to organize and to think about how you can split each task into 15 to 30-minute blocks of time. You may want to approach the easiest areas first, or, as Trapani (2010)

suggests, to start with the "live frog," or the trickiest area. Whatever your preference, schedule time to declutter these areas, spread over the week, and make a note of this schedule in your planner or calendar.

3. Before starting to declutter, gather everything you'll need, such as boxes, marker pens, cleaning supplies, and so on. In particular, gather five boxes and label them "keep here," "belongs somewhere else," "toss," "donate," and "not sure." If you think one of these boxes isn't going to get any use—for example, it's unlikely you're going to donate anything on your desk's stationary shelf—you can make do with fewer boxes. Customize your process to fit what works for you.

4. When your scheduled time to declutter comes around, set a timer for five minutes under the allotted time and start sorting the area into your five boxes. The items that you want to keep and belong in that area go in the "keep here" box; the items that you want to keep but belong elsewhere go in the "belong somewhere else" box; the items you want to throw out go in the "toss" box; the items you want to donate to charity go in the "donate" box; and the items you can't quickly sort into one of the other boxes go in the "not sure" box.

5. When the timer ends, stop decluttering and deal with the contents of your five boxes. Items in the "keep here" box can go back to what is now a hopefully decluttered area. Items in the "belong somewhere else" box should be put where they belong (don't worry about tidying that area, because presumably, you'll have scheduled to do that at another time in the week). Items in the "toss" box can be recycled or thrown in the trash, and items in the "donate" box can be put somewhere where you'll remember (perhaps by your bag if you're at your desk, or by the front door of your home). Finally, close up the "not sure" box and put it somewhere out of the way.

6. A few months later, open up your "not sure" box and have a look through the items. If you haven't needed them in a few months, chances are that you don't need them, and they can be tossed or donated. On the other hand, if you have needed them in the last few months, that's a good sign that you want to keep them: Put those items where they belong.

7. Work through all the areas of your space, using steps 4-7, according to

your schedule. Repeat the whole process routinely to keep on top of your clutter and prevent it from building up.

It may seem like a lot at first, but once you get into the habit of decluttering your space, the task of tidying up will become easier and quicker. After all, if you are regularly decluttering, less clutter will accumulate, which means that tidying up will take less time. In addition, it's worth thinking about strategies for reducing the amount of clutter you acquire in the first place. Think about what tends to cause a mess in your spaces. If it's paper and mail, it might be worth scheduling time to go through your mail regularly and to switch to paperless forms of contact as much as possible. This will stop mail from piling up and causing clutter. CHADD (n.d.-a) also recommends taking scans or photos of documents so you don't have to store physical copies: You can store the digital copies on your phone or computer, which is often easier to organize.

Relatedly, you may find that your desk is getting cluttered with paperwork belonging to different tasks. This is a sign that you are taking on too much. Try to focus on finishing one project at a time and completing a task before starting a new one. You may need to learn how to say no to unnecessary tasks that take up your time and attention. Similarly, if you are in the habit of forgetting to tidy up spills or messes, Segal and Smith (2022) suggest that you should commit to acting immediately: If a decluttering or tidying task can be done in less than two minutes, it's a good idea to do it in on the spot, rather than putting it off and inevitably forgetting about it altogether.

When it comes to other kinds of clutter, like noise and your email inbox, we have already talked about a few strategies. Scheduling some time to go through your emails (and by this, I mean *literally* scheduling the time in your day planner) can help avoid a build-up of messages, and apps like Chuck can help you when the project starts to feel unmanageable. When it comes to noise, try to control your environment as much as is practical. If you're at home and you need to focus, you might consider setting your phone to send incoming calls directly to your voicemail: Just make sure that you schedule some time to check your voicemail, otherwise you'll start missing important messages. You may also be able to do this at work, with the understanding of your employer. Similarly, if you find yourself being distracted by people talking or just the sound of other people working, you might be able to take steps to find a quieter place to work. If you're in an office, it's worth talking to your boss about finding such a space, whether that just be a corner desk or a quiet room for yourself.

By decluttering, you'll avoid draining your attention and forgetting important tasks. The ADDitude Editors (2022) also offer a few helpful tips for tackling the forgetfulness that often comes with ADHD. The key, as ever, is routine and habit. If you don't have a small shelf or table by the front door of your home, consider adding one and making it the place for essential items like your wallet, keys, and (if you don't wear them permanently) your eyeglasses. Get in the habit of always putting your essential items on the table by the front door. If you build this into your routine, you'll never have to worry about losing these items ever again. Additionally, if that's not working for you, consider attaching electronic fobs to essential items that connect to a base unit. Whenever you lose an item, you can press a button on the base unit and follow the sound to your missing item.

The ADDitude Editors (2022) also suggest that how you sort your space can be an effective way of dealing with forgetfulness and trouble finding items. It's an excellent strategy to store items that are often used together in the same space. For example, wrapping and packing paper, scissors, and tape are often used together: With this in mind, try to store these items in the same place to keep your things organized and easy to find.

Managing Your Time and Staying Organized

Next, let's talk about organization and time management. We've already discussed the importance of day planners, but I want to really stress this point: If you don't have a day planner, whether you use an app, Google Calendar, or pen and paper, it's important to start using one today. A day planner is essential for someone with ADHD who is struggling to manage their executive functions and stay organized. Again, it's vital to build in a routine of checking your day planner, so you get used to referring to it and it starts becoming second nature to use it. Don't worry if it takes a little bit of time to get used to it: This is why it's important to foster the habit and commit to checking your planner at least three times a day.

Referring more specifically to time management, Segal and Smith (2022) suggest that it's worth investing in a watch if you don't already wear one. Try to get in the habit of checking the time before starting a new task. This can build in constant awareness of the time and helps you remain focused without becoming hyper-focused beyond the point of sensible time management. Remember that a common symptom of ADHD is underestimating the length of time it takes to complete a task. With that in mind, if you are often finding yourself rushed or running out of time, it might be worth consciously adding extra time to your estimates of how long it will take to finish a project. This habit also helps you avoid becoming overscheduled with too many tasks because you will be building in some breathing room to help you manage and stay organized.

CHADD (n.d.-c) recommends the following steps that should be built into a habit to help you manage your time:

1. Select your planner of choice. Pen and paper planners have the advantage of being easily accessible and can be kept visible at all times to prompt you to use them, but also have the disadvantage of being more easily misplaced when compared to apps or computer-based planners. Choose whatever suits you best.
2. When you have chosen your preferred planner, enter your

information. This should include contact information for people that you regularly contact, as well as contact information for medical professionals and other emergency contacts.

3. Build the habit of always carrying your planner. If you are using an app, this can be a little easier as your planner will be on your phone. However, if it's a pen and paper planner, you can still commit to carrying it with you in your bag or (if it's small) in a pocket.

4. Find a safe place to put your planner when you are not carrying it around. It's important to choose one place so that you know where to look when you can't find it. Furthermore, it's important to commit to always putting your planner in that location when it's not on your person: Otherwise, when you go to look for it, it could be anywhere!

5. Schedule for yourself a daily planning session, where you enter the day's tasks into your planner. As you get into the habit of using your planner, you may be able to ease off on this, as you will get into the routine of adding to your planner as you go along. However, at the start, it is important to schedule the time and commit to it.

6. Commit to referring to your planner no less than three times a day. As we've noted, great times to check your planner are first thing in the morning, at noon or lunchtime, and in the early evening to double-check that there isn't something that still needs doing. Of course, if you end up checking your daily planner more frequently, that's great as well.

7. Make your day planner your calendar for everything. The more able you are to put all your organizational information in one place, the more effective your habit of using the day planner will be. If you're using an app like Todoist, you can split different areas of your life into different tabs: Experiment with what works for you.

CHADD (n.d.-c) also notes that your planner can be an excellent "brain dump" for intrusive thoughts. Rather than be distracted by intrusive thoughts that bounce around your head, you can write them down in your planner and come back to them later in the day, as appropriate.

Scheduling your time can also help you break down big tasks into smaller tasks, which will help prevent procrastination. Most of us are more likely to procrastinate before a big, daunting task. By breaking it down into sections in your day planner, and scheduling each section accordingly, you can avoid the task seeming daunting and break down the psychological barriers that otherwise encourage you to procrastinate.

Connectedly, consider breaking down tasks into 25-30-minute chunks so that they more naturally fit the pattern of the Pomodoro Technique. We've discussed the Pomodoro Technique a few times in this book, which Drake (2021) notes was invented by Francesco Cirillo in the late 1980s. For one last time, let's consider how the Pomodoro Technique works, in detailed stages:

1. Select a task that you want to complete.
2. Take a timer and set it to 25 minutes. A quick Google search for "Pomodoro timer" will also bring up websites that do this for you (these websites will also time your breaks).
3. Commit to focusing on your task for those 25 minutes, and work continuously until the timer stops.
4. When the 25 minutes is up, pause and make a note on a piece of paper to show that you've completed one Pomodoro cycle. Again, many resources online will keep track of your cycles for you.
5. Take a 5-minute break. If you struggle with symptoms of restlessness or fidgeting, consider getting up from your desk or having a stretch.
6. Set your timer for another Pomodoro cycle (25 minutes) and repeat steps 3-5.
7. After you have completed four Pomodoro cycles, take a longer 15-30-minute break.

The Pomodoro Technique is effective at managing both symptoms of distractibility and hyperfocus. It avoids distractibility because it helps you focus for 25 minutes at a time. Meanwhile, it avoids hyperfocus on procrastination activities because your breaks are carefully scheduled and timed. It is also customizable. You can amend the length of cycles as suits you. If you are feeling focused on your work when the timer indicates that it is time for a break, you can make the cycle a little longer. However, Drake (2021) suggests that you should avoid amending the Pomodoro Technique to take longer breaks, as this can make it harder to mentally transition between work and breaks. Similarly, you should be careful about making the cycles too long: Qi et al. (2019) note that, even if you feel focused, sustaining your attention for too long can lead to mental fatigue and an increased likelihood of making mistakes.

Managing Your Money and Other Tips

Now, let's talk about money management. If you have combined or hyperactive/impulsive type ADHD, the chances are that you can sometimes be impulsive when it comes to spending. If you think you are at risk of this becoming a problem, it's important to take steps now to avoid the accruement of debt. Segal and Smith (2022) suggest that you can tackle impulse shopping by switching to cash (or a debit card with strict controls to prevent overdraft spending) and leaving your credit cards at home. This means that you can't spend more than the cash in your pocket, which prevents the worst excesses of spending.

Relatedly, consider cutting up all but one credit card, to stop your credit card debt from getting out of hand. It's still a good idea to keep one credit card around, as this can help you build your credit score and help you handle emergency expenses, but you'll want to resist using it as much as possible.

Finally, think about your patterns of behavior and spending. If there's a particular place or store that you can't resist spending at, consider consciously avoiding that place. For example, if you find the aromas of your local food court irresistible, avoid the food court altogether to prevent yourself from ever having to resist those tempting smells.

In addition to the strategies we've discussed in this chapter, the ADDitude Editors (2022) provide some miscellaneous tips for boosting your executive function and improving your organizational skills. Why not try some of them today?

- Invite friends and family to your home—it will force you to tidy your home ahead of their visit.

- Keep a document "hotspot" for time-sensitive documents.

- Hang up a list of daily tasks in a spot you often see, such as the inside of the front door or on the fridge.

● Write down important to-do items on brightly colored paper, to attract your attention and stop you from forgetting.

● When you tidy up the dining room table, set it with placemats and cutlery at the same time: It'll prevent you from putting stuff on it and making a mess before dinner.

● Write notes for yourself and put them in your pocket—whenever you reach into your pocket, you'll get a reminder of the note.

● Never buy something on the day you see it: Wait a few days, and if you still want it, buy it then.

● Practice mindfulness or meditation exercises first thing in the morning. A quick search on YouTube can find a variety of guided mindfulness exercises to help you get started.

● If you're impulsively tempted to say something personal to someone, try mentally erasing their face: This can help you address the problem, rather than the person, and prevent hurtful, blurted-out comments.

● Listen to audiobooks or music to improve your focus.

● Turn an imaginary key in your pocket to "lock" your mouth and prevent you from blurting out something impulsive.

● Keep a small, plastic baggie in your pocket or glove compartment of your car to store receipts.

Jessica McCabe, actress and founder of the popular YouTube channel *How to ADHD*, is a big believer in using strategies and habits to help boost her executive functions. She was diagnosed when she was 12 years old and has had a lifetime of trying different strategies to see what works and doesn't work for her. She has experimented a lot—once, she quit medication, before later discovering that this was a bad idea!

Though her medication was essential for her to function properly, Jessica wasn't satisfied with her treatment. As she puts it: "as I hit my early 30s, still waiting tables and struggling with my acting career, and after many failed relationships, I decided meds were not enough" (Bailey, 2022). Her YouTube channel, founded in January 2016, is a testament to this new attitude. Jessica uses her platform to discuss different strategies and to compile an inventory of tools and tips that might help her. For example, Jessica is a big believer in daily meditation and the use of fidget toys, to help calm her mind and keep her hands busy. Jessica is a perfect example of how executive function in the ADHD brain can be supported and boosted with healthy habits and strategies. So, give it a try. It's never too early to start managing your symptoms of ADHD.

Chapter 7:
The ADHD Brain

Chris was diagnosed with ADHD when he was 43. He learned about his ADHD after his 16-year-old daughter was diagnosed with the condition. Chris describes the diagnosis as a "relief" (Thriving With ADHD, n.d.). He could finally give context to his troubles with procrastination and paying attention. Chris explains how he used to feel: "Like I was watching an old TV with lots of static. I could still see the picture and kind of hear what was being said, but it took real effort/concentration to work through all that noise" (Thriving With ADHD, n.d.).

After being diagnosed, Chris has been taking Ritalin and is working with his doctors on getting the right dosage. His medication is helping: "Now, it's like the picture is finely tuned" (Thriving With ADHD, n.d.). Furthermore, Chris has experienced relief when it comes to his social anxiety and introversion: "I feel a lot more comfortable in social situations and have even found myself looking forward to my work function" (Thriving With ADHD, n.d.).

Like Chris, many people who are diagnosed with ADHD in adulthood are learning about the condition through their children's diagnoses. As society starts to have a better understanding and awareness of ADHD, schools are getting better at identifying symptoms of the condition so that their pupils can get the help they need. Meanwhile, the parents are realizing that what has been diagnosed as ADHD in their children mirrors their own way of thinking and patterns of behavior. The NHS (2021) reports that there is likely a genetic factor to ADHD: It runs in families, so if a child has ADHD, it is not uncommon for one of their parents to have it as well.

It is not currently possible to diagnose ADHD on the basis of a brain scan. Sinfield (2022) notes that brain scans can be limited because they only show the state of the brain at the moment that the scan is being performed. For a diagnosis of ADHD, it's important to get a picture of your life over several months and years, so a brain scan snapshot is insufficient. On the other hand, brain scans and other imaging techniques have been used to throw more light on the condition, and to chart neurological differences between brains unaffected by ADHD, and the ADHD brain.

Sinfield (2022) reports that there are three broad areas of difference in the ADHD brain, relating to structure, function, and chemistry. To get a better understanding of the neurological underpinnings of ADHD, we'll take a look at each in turn.

The Structure of the ADHD Brain

The structure of the brain refers to its overall size and the relative size of its parts. Hoogman et al. (2017) find that the volume of the ADHD brain is smaller in five subcortical areas and that the overall volume of the ADHD brain is smaller. In addition, the amygdala and hippocampus in the ADHD brain tend to be smaller, which are the areas of the brain that are involved in emotional processing and impulsivity. These differences in the structure of the ADHD brain when compared to non-ADHD brains are more marked in childhood, suggesting that parts of the ADHD brain mature and grow at a slower rate (and never fully mature in adulthood).

It's worth making clear at this point that there is no link between intelligence and the general size of your brain, but that the relative size of different areas of the brain can impact different aspects of cognition. For example, the ADHD brain primarily develops more slowly in the frontal lobe, which Watson (2021) notes is responsible for executive functions such as impulse control, attentiveness, and memory. In particular, a smaller frontal lobe can impact your working memory, which is "the small amount of information that your mind holds as you're working to complete a task" (Watson, 2021). Kofler et al. (2020) have found that the majority of children with ADHD have impaired working memory, while Matt et al. (2013) have replicated this result in adults with ADHD.

Interestingly, it is less obvious whether there is a link between ADHD and impaired long-term memory. Skodzik et al. (2016) suggest that there is some statistical link, but that this is probably explained by difficulties in acquiring long-term memory techniques in childhood, rather than a fixed limitation of the ADHD brain. Because having ADHD can make it difficult to learn new things, children with ADHD may have never acquired the long-term memory techniques that people without ADHD use every day. Similarly, a research review conducted by Callahan et al. (2017) concludes that there is no clear link between ADHD and cognitive disorders such as dementia. Though research is still ongoing, it may be that ADHD only impacts your short-term, working memory, which you may recognize from your own experiences of living with ADHD.

Additionally, there is evidence that ADHD is linked to the slower development of the cerebellum (Shaw et al., 2018). Hallowell (2021-b) writes that the cerebellum is at the back and base of the brain, and, despite its small size, contains up to 70% of all the neurons in your brain. The cerebellum is very important: The Cleveland Clinic (n.d.) writes that it "helps coordinate and regulate a wide range of functions and processes in both your brain and body," such as balance, learning, judging size or distance, and your sense of time.

The Functioning of the ADHD Brain

Let's talk next about brain function. Brain function refers to where blood flows in the brain when higher blood flow in a particular area of the brain indicates higher activity. Imaging techniques such as functional magnetic resonance imaging (fMRI) work on this principle, detecting relative levels of blood flow in your brain. When it comes to thinking about ADHD, research by Kim et al. (2010) shows that there is decreased blood flow to some prefrontal areas in the ADHD brain. These prefrontal areas are responsible for executive functions, which is reflected in the difficulties many people with ADHD have when it comes to time management and organization. These findings have been replicated with other imaging techniques, such as positron emission tomography (PET) and single-photon emission computer tomography (SPECT).

Additionally, imaging techniques have found an association between ADHD and dysfunctional brain connectivity. Put in layman's terms, this means that the connections between different parts of the ADHD brain work differently than in the non-ADHD brain. Resting-state MRIs have found that symptoms of hyperactivity and restlessness are associated with increased functional connectivity between certain areas of the ADHD brain (Sörös et al., 2019). Relatedly, Mazaheri et al. (2010) find that children with ADHD do not have the same connections between the frontal cortex of the brain and the visual processing area as in the non-ADHD brain. This suggests that the ADHD brain literally processes information differently when compared to the non-ADHD brain.

Recent research has also exposed a connection between ADHD and the default mode network (DMN) of the brain, which Hallowell (2021-a) describes as "the demon of ADHD." The DMN includes parts of the inferior parietal lobe, the hippocampus, the medial prefrontal cortex, the amygdala, and the posterior cingulate cortex. When your brain is not engaged in a task, the DMN is more active than other parts of the brain. It seems to be linked to ruminating or musing about past events. By contrast, the task-positive network (TPN) of the brain is more active when you are giving attention to a task. In a non-ADHD brain, the DMN and the TPN are reciprocal. When the non-ADHD brain focuses on a task, the TPN activates and the DMN reduces in activity, and vice versa when there is no task to focus on. However, in the ADHD brain, the DMN does not work reciprocally with the TPN: When you try to pay attention to a task, the TPN activates, but the DMN doesn't reduce its activity (Silberstein et al., 2016). This puts them in direct competition. Hallowell (2021-a) notes that this "provides a neurological explanation for what those of us who have ADHD feel so often—a persistent, magnetic pull away from the task at hand into distraction."

Unfortunately, activation of the DMN can produce unpleasant or cringeworthy memories. The hippocampus, which is responsible for memory, is an active part of the DMN, while the medial prefrontal cortex "projects the repetition of these horrible moments into the future" (Hallowell, 2021-a). This can, in turn, affect your self-esteem and undermine your confidence.

The Chemistry of the ADHD Brain

Next, let's consider the brain chemistry of the ADHD brain. Brain chemistry refers to the activity of neurotransmitters, which are the chemical messengers of your brain. You may have heard of dopamine, which is a neurotransmitter involved in the pleasure and reward centers of the brain. Del Campo et al. (2011) find that ADHD is associated with dysregulation of the dopamine system, which in this case means that there are lower levels of dopamine and noradrenaline in the ADHD brain. Similarly, Kollins et al. (2014) find that dysregulation of the dopamine system can produce symptoms of ADHD.

As a neurotransmitter for the pleasure and reward centers of the brain, dopamine is very important for regulating aspects of learning. This is because motivation is very important to learning because without motivation you will get distracted or lose interest before acquiring and storing new information. Meanwhile, motivation is linked to the pleasure and reward centers of the brain, which in turn relies on dopamine and noradrenaline. Heyl (2022) reports that people with ADHD have a higher dopamine transporter density (DTD), which results in lower levels of dopamine in the brain.

ADHD medication works by reducing the dysregulation of the dopamine system. Central nervous system (CNS) stimulant medications, like methylphenidate (also known as Ritalin) or amphetamine-based stimulants (also known as Adderall), work by increasing the production of dopamine and noradrenaline in the brain.

Sometimes, stimulant medication can be ineffective, or produce side effects that are too severe to justify continuing their use. These potential side effects include increased blood pressure, a loss of appetite, trouble sleeping, stomach aches, or changes to your mood, such as making you feel irritable, anxious, tense, aggressive, or depressed. Where stimulant medication is not working, doctors can prescribe non-stimulant medications that work by increasing levels of noradrenaline only. With this in mind, it's always important to talk about any side effects you are experiencing from your medication with your doctor: Alternative medications do exist.

Other Science-Based Ways to Treat Your ADHD

In addition to medication, people with ADHD can manage their symptoms by doing exercises that help strengthen neural connections to areas of the brain that are structurally or functionally affected by the condition. One of the most magical things about our brains is encapsulated in neuroplasticity: The ability of our brain to form new connections and, in the case of neurogenesis, even form new neurons. Neuroplasticity is at its height in childhood—explaining why it's often easier to learn a language or an instrument if you start young—but it continues into adulthood and throughout your entire life. This means that it's possible to take steps to change your brain function and reduce symptoms of your ADHD.

For example, Hallowell (2021-b) recommends doing regular balance exercises, such as standing on one leg. This stimulates your cerebellum, which prompts your brain to strengthen neural connections to that part of the brain. When you have mastered standing on one leg, try doing it with your eyes closed to improve your balance further. You can also buy a cheap balance board online, which helps you practice and strengthens your core.

Similarly, you can take steps to activate certain areas of the brain with simple behavioral exercises. Let's think again about the default mode network (DMN), which, in the ADHD brain, remains active and in competition against the task-positive network (TPN) when you try to give your attention to a task. Hallowell (2021-a) reports that simple breathing exercises can be effective in strengthening the TPN, helping you focus and pay attention. The key is to make the breathing exercise a task that you need to pay attention to: Hallowell suggests picking a pattern of breathing, such as 6-3-8-3 (inhaling for six beats, holding for three beats, exhaling for eight beats, holding for three beats, and repeat). A few cycles of this breathing pattern can help activate the TPN and break you out of the DMN.

Relatedly, you can use techniques from cognitive behavioral therapy (CBT) to manage symptoms of negative thinking that can be produced by the DMN.

The basic principle of CBT is the cognitive cycle: The idea that our thoughts, behaviors, feelings, and physical sensations are intrinsically linked, and feed into each other. To take a simple example, if you feel hot and uncomfortable, this might make you feel irritable, which might result in you behaving more impulsively, or thinking negative thoughts about your situation.

The key thought behind the cognitive cycle is that we can use this interconnectedness to our advantage. We are used to letting our feelings rule the roost: How we feel has a powerful impact on our thoughts and behaviors. However, it's hard to change your feelings directly. If you've ever been told to "just stop worrying," you can probably appreciate what I mean. On the other hand, our thoughts and behaviors are more tractable. The principle behind CBT, then, is making gentle modifications to our thoughts and behaviors to positively influence our feelings and physical sensations: Reversing the normal direction of influence and feeling better as a result. For example, studies show that the simple act of forcing yourself to smile can have a positive effect on your mood (Coles et al., 2019).

Do you remember the types of disordered thinking from Chapter 5? The strategies outlined there for managing disordered thinking are based on CBT. They are designed to help you get better at realizing when you're in the grips of disordered thinking and to train you to practice more positive thinking. You can use these techniques to take the sting out of negative memories that might be produced by the overactive DMN.

Relatedly, you might consider talking to your therapist about acceptance and commitment therapy (ACT), which incorporates elements of both behavioral therapy and CBT. ACT involves facing your challenges directly, and gently modifying the way you think and behave to foster more positive ways of approaching life. Psychology Today (n.d.) writes that "ACT aims to develop and expand psychological flexibility. Psychological flexibility encompasses emotional openness and the ability to adapt your thoughts and behaviors to better align with your values and goals." There are six "core processes" that help promote healthy, psychological flexibility:

1. **Acceptance:** Instead of attempting to deny or repress your thoughts,

acceptance means acknowledging and embracing the way you feel.

2. **Cognitive defusion:** Achieved through mindfulness techniques, such as learning to observe your own thoughts without judgment, cognitive defusion involves distancing yourself from thoughts and feelings that distress you.

3. **Being present:** By remaining mindful of the present moment, you can observe your own thoughts and feelings without judgment and start to see events more objectively. In turn, this can help you behave more appropriately in response to them.

4. **Self as context:** The idea of self as context is that we are more than our thoughts, feelings, and experiences. This can be important in helping us to find self-acceptance if we have negative thoughts or feelings.

5. **Values:** By choosing personal values and trying to live by those values, we can avoid negative or disruptive behaviors.

6. **Committed Action:** When we commit to action, this means we take concrete steps to work towards positive change. Psychology Today (n.d.) notes that "this may involve goal setting, exposure to difficult thoughts or experiences, and skill development."

The main thought behind ACT is that it is counterproductive to attempt to control negative feelings because suppressing our thoughts and feelings tends to make them stronger. Instead, ACT techniques ask you to address and accept your feelings, and then give you the tools for processing negative feelings and making positive changes. If this sounds like something you'd be interested in, it's worth talking to your therapist or doctor to start ACT today.

Meanwhile, specific treatment techniques are being developed to take advantage of childhood neuroplasticity. Abbey (2021) has produced a gamified program to help train reading and cognitive skills in his patients. Similarly, Lansbergen et al. (2011) have used electroencephalographic (EEF) biofeedback to help children learn new focusing techniques. In this case, the researchers used EEF biofeedback to measure brain waves and constantly monitor a child's level of attention. This level of attention was then linked to a gamified task: To keep a plane flying in the air on a screen. When the EEF biofeedback indicated that the child was getting distracted, the plane would start to dive, or the screen would start going dark. This taught the child to keep focusing so they could keep the plane flying.

These treatments are still in development and will probably focus on treating ADHD in children. However, there are still steps you can take other than medication to help manage your symptoms. For example, it's worth paying attention to what you're eating. In Chapter 3, we discussed the importance of a nutritious, protein-rich diet for managing the symptoms of ADHD, but there are also specific chemicals in food that you might want to avoid. Story (2019) writes that some food colorings and preservatives have been found to exacerbate ADHD symptoms, such as:

- FD&C Yellow No.5: Often found in pickles, yogurt, granola bars, and cereal

- FD&C Yellow No.6: Often found in soft drink, candy, icing, breadcrumbs and cereal

- FD&C Yellow No.10: Often found in sorbets, smoked haddock, and juices

- FD&C Red No.40: Often found in children's medications, gelatin desserts, ice cream, and soft drinks

- Sodium benzoate: Often found in salad dressings, fruit juices, and carbonated drinks

Relatedly, Story (2019) recommends avoiding potential allergens, which have also been linked to worsening the symptoms of ADHD. Meanwhile, there is mixed evidence that certain supplements, such as magnesium, zinc, vitamin B-6, and L-carnitine, can improve the symptoms of ADHD, and that herbs like passionflower, ginseng, and ginkgo can help calm hyperactivity. If you are considering taking supplements, however, it's always worth talking to your doctor first.

You can also manage your symptoms by enjoying the fresh outdoors. Taylor and Kuo (2009) found that children with ADHD showed a marked improvement in their concentration skills after spending time outside for just 20 minutes. Tillman et al. (2018) replicated these findings. Many people with ADHD also report that practicing yoga or tai chi helps improve their symptoms and aids them with their focus and concentration. This is supported by clinical evidence (Chou and Huag, 2017, Herbert and Esparham, 2017). Relatedly, Modesto-Lowe et al. (2015) find that practicing mindfulness is an effective method for improving your attention. You can find any number of guided yoga or mindfulness exercises online: Why not try one today?

You may also find that music can help soothe symptoms of ADHD. Rodgers (2022) gives the case of Arizona congresswoman Gabrielle Giffords as an example of the therapeutic impact of music on brain trauma. Giffords survived a gunshot wound to her left temple in January 2011. Because of damage to the left hemisphere of her brain, she was initially unable to sleep, but music therapy was used as part of her recovery to help her regain these functions. Remarkably, she was able to sing a word before she could speak it.

Music can provide structure that helps you maintain focus. Rodgers (2022) notes that "music is rhythm, rhythm is structure, and structure is soothing to an ADHD brain struggling to regulate itself to stay on a linear path." Another benefit of music is that it commonly activates the dopamine system, increasing dopamine levels that are typically lower in the ADHD brain.

You will also find it helpful to regularly exercise: Especially if you have been diagnosed with hyperactive/impulsive or combined type ADHD. Exercise can help you use up excess energy that might otherwise lead to distractions or restlessness.

Finally, it's worth thinking about all the other strategies and tips provided in this book. All of them are designed to help you manage your symptoms, and every method is compatible and mutually supportive. By committing to these healthy habits, you are on the first step to living a happier and more fulfilling life with ADHD.

A Final Testimony

Let's finish things off with a positive story of ADHD, provided anonymously to ADHD Awareness (2022):

> I have found that being honest about my ADHD has been the most freeing and positive part of being diagnosed. Prior to being diagnosed (at 30 years old), I was told I shouldn't self-diagnose, and to trust that the medical professionals know better than I do. My belief in myself, and my self-advocacy has created monumental change in the way I trust my own instincts but has also given me a wind of confidence that I can take control of my mental health. I have been diagnosed as clinically depressed, with anxiety and a panic disorder for over 10 years, and even with all the therapy and different medications, I have not had this clarity about myself (para. 2).

By picking up and reading this book, you have shown that you are ready to take control of your mental health. Use that inner strength and confidence to practice the strategies and tips laid out in the book, and to foster positive habits that will help you manage the symptoms of your ADHD. By managing and then harnessing those symptoms, you will be able to do more than simply cope with ADHD: You will be able to turn ADHD into your very own superpower. ADHD is part of what makes you special and unique, but it doesn't define you. Many individuals with ADHD lead happy, productive, and fulfilling lives. So, stay positive, and don't give up.

Please Rate and Review!

If you have enjoyed this book, it would mean the world to me if you could rate and review the book now.

By rating and giving honest feedback, you can help this book find a wider audience and reach more people who are living with ADHD. The power is in your hands, and you can make such a difference. Best of all, it only takes a minute or two.

I want to hear what you have to say about your experience of living with ADHD. Because of the stigma that sometimes surrounds ADHD, too many of us are suffering in silence. So, I want to hear your stories, whether they are happy or sad. I want to hear how you have harnessed your inner resilience to foster new habits and strategies. I want to hear your own suggestions for those tips and methods that have helped you thrive.

I'm ready to listen: All you need to do is write.

Thank you.

References

AADD-UK. (n.d.). *Comorbidities.* AADD-UK. https://aadduk.org/symptoms-diagnosis-treatment/comorbidities/

Abraham, A., Windmann, S., Siefen, R., Daum, I. & Güntürkün, O. (2006). Creative thinking in adolescents with attention deficit hyperactivity disorder (ADHD). *Child Neuropsychology, 12*(2), 111-123.

Ackerman, C. E. (2018, April 3). *Growth mindset vs fixed.* Positive Psychology. https://positivepsychology.com/growth-mindset-vs-fixed-mindset/

Adamis, D., Flynn, C., Wrigley, M., Gavin, B., & McNicholas, F. (2022). ADHD in adults: A systematic review and meta-analysis of prevalence studies in outpatient psychiatric clinics. *Journal of Attention Disorders.*

adda. (n.d.) *Top 5 potential benefits of ADHD for employees.* Attention Deficit Disorder Association. https://adhdatwork.add.org/potential-benefits-of-having-an-adhd-employee/

ADDitude Editors. (2022, July 13). *ADHD coping strategies you haven't tried yet.* ADDitude. https://www.additudemag.com/dealing-with-adhd-80-coping-strategies/

ADHD Awareness (2022). *ADHD stories.* https://www.adhdawarenessmonth.org/category/stories/

Adult ADHD Clinic. (n.d.) *Married with children.* https://adhdclinic.co.uk/2018/12/18/married-with-children-philips-adhd-story/

Advanced Psychiatry Associates. (2021, May 11). *Strategies for adults living with ADHD.* https://advancedpsychiatryassociates.com/resources/blog/strategies-for-adults-living-with-adhd/

American Psychiatric Association. (n.d.). *What is ADHD?* Psychiatry.org. https://www.psychiatry.org/patients-families/adhd/what-is-adhd

American Psychiatric Association. (2022). *Diagnostic and statistical manual of mental disorders* (5th ed., text rev.).

Bailey, E. (2022, January 21). *When it's more than ADHD.* ADDitude. https://www.additudemag.com/slideshows/avoid-adhd-misdiagnosis-related-disorders-overview/

Bailey, E. (2022, March 31). *"My ADHD diagnosis connected the dots in my life."* ADDitude. https://www.additudemag.com/adult-adhd-diagnosis/

Baroncini-Moe, S. (2013). *Business in blue jeans: How to have a successful business on your own terms, in your own style.* Sound Wisdom.

Bilkey, T. [Global News]. (2018, February 19). *Can adults have ADHD? A psychiatrist explains the symptoms* [Video]. YouTube. https://www.youtube.com/watch?v=mv-BME1SmTA&ab_channel=GlobalNews

Bloodworth, J. (2021, April 30). *Diagnosed with adult ADHD age 37. Here's my story.* The ADHD Centre. https://www.adhdcentre.co.uk/diagnosed-with-adult-adhd-age-37

Blunt, K. (2022, July 9). *"Learning to let go of ADHD what-ifs and regrets."* ADDitude. https://www.additudemag.com/how-to-let-things-go-regret-late-adhd-diagnosis/

Bonior, A. (2019, July 25). *What is rejection sensitive dysphoria?* Psychology Today. https://www.psychologytoday.com/gb/blog/friendship-20/201907/what-is-rejection-sensitive-dysphoria

Boot, N., Nevicka, B., Bass, M. (2017). Creativity in ADHD: Goal-directed motivation and domain specificity. *Journal of Attention Disorders, 24*(13).

Braaten, E. (n.d.). *Is there an ADHD spectrum?* Understood. https://www.understood.org/en/articles/is-there-an-adhd-spectrum

Callahan, B. L., Bierstone, D., Stuss, D. T. & Black, S. E. (2017). Adult ADHD: Risk factor for dementia or phenotypic mimic? *Frontiers in Aging Neuroscience, 9,* 260.

CHADD. (n.d.-a). *Organizing the home and office space.* https://chadd.org/for-adults/organizing-the-home-and-office-space/

CHADD. (n.d.-b). *Relationships & social skills.* CHADD.org. https://chadd.org/for-adults/relationships-social-skills/

CHADD. (n.d.-c). *Time management and ADHD: Day planners.* https://chadd.org/for-adults/time-management-planner/

Chan, E. S. M., Groves, N. B., Marsh, C. L., Miller, C. E., Richmond, K. P., Kofler, M. J. (2021). Are there resilient children with ADHD? *Journal of Attention Disorders.*

Cherry, K. (2021, September 25). *What are the benefits of having ADHD?* Verywell Mind. https://www.verywellmind.com/adhd-benefits-advantages-challenges-and-tips-5199254

Chou, C.-C. & Huag, C.-J. (2017). Effects of an 8-week yoga program on sustained attention and discrimination function in children with attention deficit hyperactivity disorder. *PeerJ,* *5*(e2883).

Christina, (n.d.). *5 mood tracker bullet journal ideas for mental well-being.* Zen Art Supplies. https://www.zenartsupplies.co/blogs/inspiration/mood-tracker-bullet-journal-ideas

Cleveland Clinic (n.d.) *Cerebellum.* https://my.clevelandclinic.org/health/body/23418-cerebellum#[1]

Coles, N. A., Larsen, J. T. & Lench, H. C. (2019). A meta-analysis of the facial feedback literature: Effects of facial feedback on emotional experience are small and variable. *Psychological Bulletin, 145*(6), 610-651.

Del Campo, N., Chamberlain, S. R., Sahakian, B. J., Robbins, T. W. (2011). The roles of dopamine and noradrenaline in the pathophysiology and treatment of attention-deficit/hyperactivity disorder. *Biological Psychiatry, 69*(12), 145-157.

Drake, K. (2021, August 31). *Pomodoro technique may aid folks with ADHD.* PsychCentral. https://psychcentral.com/adhd/how-to-adapt-the-pomodoro-technique-adhd#1[2]

Ferguson, S. (2021, March 3). *Tips for living with ADHD.* PsychCentral. https://psychcentral.com/adhd/living-with-adhd

---

1. https://my.clevelandclinic.org/health/body/23418-cerebellum#_853ae90f0351324bd73ea615e6487517__4c761f170e016836ff84498202b99827__853ae90f0351324bd73ea615e6487517_text_43ec3e5dee6e706af7766fffea512721_Your_0bcef9c45bd8a48eda1b26eb0c61c869_20cerebellum_0bcef9c45bd8a48eda1b26eb0c61c869_20is_0bcef9c45bd8a48eda1b26eb0c61c869_20part_0bcef9c45bd8a48eda1b26eb0c61c869_20of_c0cb5f0fcf239ab3d9c1fcd31fff1efc_system

2. https://psychcentral.com/adhd/how-to-adapt-the-pomodoro-technique-adhd#a5c02393e59c943d6a75a9241140faca31

Finch, S. D. (2017, July 22). *ADHD survival guide: How I stopped procrastinating and got my sh!T together.* Let's Queer Things Up. https://letsqueerthingsup.com/2017/07/22/adhd-survival-guide/

Hallowell, E. (2021, June 24). *ADHD's secret demon—and how to tame it.* ADDitude. https://www.additudemag.com/default-mode-network-adhd-brain/

Hallowell, N. [Psych Hub]. (2021-b, January 13). *How to treat ADHD (without medication)* [Video]. YouTube. https://www.youtube.com/watch?v=cvxULrV5qT4&ab_channel=PsychHub

Herbert, A. & Esparham, A. (2017). Mind-body therapy for children with attention deficit/hyperactivity disorder. *Children, 4*(5), 31.

Heyl, J. C. (2022, August 30). *The relationship between dopamine and ADHD.* Verywell Mind. https://www.verywellmind.com/the-relationship-between-dopamine-and-adhd-5267960

Hinojosa, R. (2022, July 8). *ADHD in men: Signs, symptoms, & treatments.* Choosing Therapy. https://www.choosingtherapy.com/adhd-in-men/

Ho, J., Kittleson, K. [MedCircle]. (2022, August 12). *Do you have adult ADHD inattentive type? Here are 9 hidden signs* [Video]. YouTube. https://www.youtube.com/watch?v=ToN-y8CNl-Q&ab_channel=MedCircle

Hoogman, M., Bralten, J., Hibar, D. P., et al. (2017). Subcortical brain volume differences in participants with attention deficit hyperactivity disorder in children and adults: A cross-sectional mega-analysis. *Lancet Psychiatry, 4*(4), 310-319.

Hovde, M. (2022, June 23). *All about ADHD in men.* PsychCentral. https://psychcentral.com/adhd/adhd-in-men

Kim, B. N., Kim, J. W., Kang, H., et al. (2010). Regional differences in cerebral perfusion associated with the alpha-2A-adrenergic receptor genotypes in attention deficit hyperactivity disorder. *Journal of Psychiatry and Neuroscience, 35*(5), 330-336.

Kimball, K. & Effiong, H. (2021, May 25). *Practical solutions for symptoms of ADHD with Dr. Hokehe Effiong, Healthy Parenting Connector: E130* [Video]. YouTube. https://www.youtube.com/watch?v=kPOFMfknt8w&ab_channel=KatieKimball

Kofler, M. J., Singh, L. J., Soto, E. F., Chan, E. S. M., Miller, C. E., Harmon, S. L., Spiegel, J. A. (2020). Working memory and short-term memory deficits in ADHD: A bifactor modeling approach. *Neuropsychology, 34*(6), 686-698.

Kollins, S. H. & Adcock, R. A. (2014). ADHD, Altered dopamine neurotransmission, and disrupted reinforcement processes: Implications for smoking and nicotine dependence. *Progress in Neuro-Psychopharmacology and Biological Psychiatry, 3*(52), 70-78.

Lansbergen, M. M., van Dongen-Boomsma, M., Buitelaar, J. K. & Slaats-Willemse, D. (2011). ADHD and EEF-neurofeedback: A double-blind randomized placebo-controlled feasibility study. *Journal of Neural Transmission, 118*(2), 275-284.

Low, K. (2021, September 12). *Living with ADHD: Strategies for well-being.* Verywell Mind. https://www.verywellmind.com/living-well-with-adhd-20480

Martell, D. (2018, July 9). *How I manage my ADHD without medication* [Video]. YouTube. https://www.youtube.com/watch?v=4rEwOMf_khY&ab_channel=DanMartell

Matt, A. R., Kasper, L. J., Hudec, K. L., Patros, C. H. G. (2013). Attention-deficit/hyperactivity disorder (ADHD) and working memory in adults: A meta-analytic review. *Neuropsychology, 27*(3), 287-302.

Mazaheri, A., Coffey-Corina, S., Mangun, G. R., Bekker, E. M., Berry, A. S., Corbett, B. A. (2010). Functional disconnection of frontal cortex and visual cortex in attention-deficit/hyperactivity disorder. *Biological Psychiatry, 67*(7), 617-623.

Milkman, K. (2021, November 29). *How to build a habit in 5 steps, according to science.* CNN Health. https://edition.cnn.com/2021/11/29/health/5-steps-habit-builder-wellness/index.html

Modesto-Lowe, V., Farahmand, P., Chaplin, M. & Sarro, L. (2015). Does mindfulness meditation improve attention in attention deficit hyperactivity disorder? *World Journal of Psychiatry, 5*(4), 397-403.

Montano, B. [ADHD in Adults]. (2014, January 14). *ADHD symptoms & behaviors in adults, ADHD in Adults* [Video]. YouTube. https://www.youtube.com/watch?v=lzGQ4dkyl8U&ab_channel=ADHDinAdults

Morin, A. (2022, May 4). *What is cognitive reframing?* Verywell. https://www.verywellmind.com/reframing-defined-2610419

Nall, R. (2021, January 19). *The benefits of ADHD.* Healthline. https://www.healthline.com/health/adhd/benefits-of-adhd

National Institute of Mental Health. (n.d.). *Attention-deficit/hyperactivity disorder (ADHD).* https://www.nimh.nih.gov/health/statistics/attention-deficit-hyperactivity-disorder-adhd

Neff, K. (n.d.). *Self-compassion guided practices and exercises.* Self-Compassion. https://self-compassion.org/category/exercises/#exercises

NeuroHealth. (n.d.) *The symptoms of ADHD in adult men: How ADHD manifests in adults.* https://neurohealthah.com/blog/adhd-in-adult-men/

NHS. (2021, December 24). *Attention deficit hyperactivity disorder (ADHD).* National Health Service. https://www.nhs.uk/conditions/attention-deficit-hyperactivity-disorder-adhd/

Nogrady, B. (2022, October 7). *Adult ADHD diagnosis: "You've got to relook at your entire life".* The Guardian. https://www.theguardian.com/society/2022/oct/08/adult-adhd-diagnosis-youve-got-to-relook-at-your-entire-life

Noor, A. (n.d.) *ADHD and the protection under the Americans With Disabilities Act.* Disability Resource Community. https://www.disabilityresource.org/47-adhd-and-the-protection-under-the-ada#[3]

Olivardia, R. (2022, March 31). *Anxiety? Depression? Or ADHD? It could be all three.* ADDitude. https://www.additudemag.com/adhd-anxiety-depression-the-diagnosis-puzzle-of-related-conditions/

Orlov, M. [ADHD Marriage]. (2017, May 10). *ADHD couples stories* [Video]. YouTube. https://www.youtube.com/watch?v=1mYgzdZ-WWQ&ab_channel=ADHDMarriage

Orlov, M. (2022, July 13). *For men with ADHD—and those who love them.* ADDitude. https://www.additudemag.com/adhd-men-relationship-anger-shame-communication/

Phillips, J. [TED-Ed Student Talks]. (2018, February 23). *ADHD: Finding what works for me* [Video]. YouTube. https://www.youtube.com/watch?v=Iw2QCcm0yIA&ab_channel=TED-EdStudentTalks

---

3. https://www.disabilityresource.org/47-adhd-and-the-protection-under-the-ada

Qi, P., Ru, H., Gao, L., Zhang, X., Zhou, T., Tian, Y., Thakor, N., Bezerianos, A., Li, J., Sun, Y. (2019). Neural mechanisms of mental fatigue revisited: New insights from the brain connectome. *Engineering, 5*(2), 276-286.

Rosen, D. & Pera, G. (2018, May 30). *One man's story: Growing up undiagnosed ADHD.* ADHD Roller Coaster. https://adhdrollercoaster.org/essays/one-mans-rugged-reality-of-add/

Scott, E. (2020, September 28). *How to reframe situations so they create less stress.* Verywell. https://www.verywellmind.com/cognitive-reframing-for-stress-management-3144872

Sedgwick, J. A., Merwood, A., Asherson, P. (2019). The positive aspects of attention deficit hyperactivity disorder: A qualitative investigation of successful adults with ADHD. *ADHD Attention Deficit and Hyperactivity Disorders, 11*(3), 241-253.

Segal, R. & Smith, M. (2022, December 30). *Tips for managing adult ADHD.* HelpGuide. https://www.helpguide.org/articles/add-adhd/managing-adult-adhd-attention-deficit-disorder.htm

Shaw, P., Ishii-Takahashi, A., Park, M. T., Devenyi, G. A., Zibman, C., Kasparek, S., Sudre, G., Mangalmurti, A., Hoogman, M., Tiemeier, H., von Polier, G., Shook, D., Muetzel, R., Chakravarty, M. M., Konrad, K., Durston, S. & White, T. (2018). A multicohort, longitudinal study of cerebellar development in attention deficit hyperactivity disorder. *Journal of Child Psychology and Psychiatry, 59*(10), 1114-1123.

Silberstein, R. B., Pipingas, A., Farrow, M., Levy, F. & Stough, C. K. (2016). Dopaminergic modulation of default mode network brain functional connectivity in attention deficit hyperactivity disorder. *Brain and Behavior, 6*(12).

Sinfield, J. (2022, November 14). *The ADHD vs. non-ADHD brain.* Verywell Mind. https://www.verywellmind.com/the-adhd-brain-4129396

Skodzik, T., Holling, H. & Pedersen, A. (2016). Long-term memory performance in adult ADHD: A meta-analysis. *Journal of Attention Disorders, 21*(4).

Sörös, P., Hoxhaj, E., Borel, P., et al. (2019). Hyperactivity/restlessness is associated with increased functional connectivity in adults with ADHD: A dimensional analysis of resting state fMRI. *BMC Psychiatry, 19*(1), 43.

Story, C. M. (2019, March 22). *6 natural remedies for ADHD.* Healthline. https://www.healthline.com/health/adhd/natural-remedies

Taylor, A. F. & Kuo, F. E. (2009). Children with attention deficits concentrate better after walk in the park. *Journal of Attention Disorders, 12*(5).

Thriving With ADHD. (n.d.). *You are not alone: Adults with ADHD share their stories.* https://thrivingwithadhd.com.au/blog/you-are-not-alone-adults-with-adhd-share-their-stories/

Tillmann, S., Tobin, D., Avison, W. & Gilliland, J. (2018). Mental health benefits of interactions with nature in children and teenagers: A systematic review. *Journal of Epidemiology and Community Health, 72*(10), 958-966.

Trapani, G. (2010, March 22). *Work smart: Do your worst task first (or, eat a live frog every morning).* Fast Company. https://www.fastcompany.com/1592454/work-smart-do-your-worst-task-first-or-eat-live-frog-every-morning

Watson, K. (2021, August 14). *ADHD and memory: What to know.* Healthline. https://www.healthline.com/health/adhd/adhd-memory

Weissenberger, S., Ptacek, R., Klicperova-Baker, M., et al. (2017). ADHD, lifestyles and comorbidities: A call for an holistic perspective—from medical to societal intervening factors. *Frontiers in Psychology, 8,* 454.

White, H. A. & Shah, P. (2011). Creative style and achievement in adults with attention-deficit/hyperactivity disorder. *Personality and Individual Differences, 50*(5), 673-677